422.48

422.48.

NIKE,
NURSES AND
NEON

NIKE, NURSES AND NEON

THE ANCIENT GREEK AND LATIN WORDS WE USE EVERY DAY

NIGEL P. BROWN

metro

Published by Metro, an imprint of John Blake Publishing Ltd,
3 Bramber Court, 2 Bramber Road,
London W14 9PB, England

www.blake.co.uk

First published in hardback in 2008

ISBN 978 1 84454 650 3

British Library Cataloguing-in-Publication Data:

A catalogue record for this book is available from the British Library.

Design by www.envydesign.co.uk

Printed and bound in Great Britain by Creative Print & Design,
Blaina, Wales

1 3 5 7 9 10 8 6 4 2

Papers used by John Blake Publishing are natural, recyclable products
made from wood grown in sustainable forests. The manufacturing
processes conform to the environmental regulations of the country
of origin.

Every attempt has been made to contact the relevant copyright-holders,
but some were unobtainable. We would be grateful if the appropriate
people could contact us.

Dedication

(Lat. *dedicare* = to declare down)

A dedication is an entreaty from the speaker on the soap box to his or her supporters in the audience to be helpful.

My clique of helpful supporters has been:-

Family: Martin, Victoria, Nicholas and Thea.
Bouncers (as in, bounce ideas off): Duncan and Ollie.
Agent: Sheila Ableman.
Editors: Daniel Bunyard and Clive Hebard.

...plus David Stevens without whom this book would never have been conceived.

One day on a chairlift in the ski-ing resort of Lech, in Austria, David pointed to an area of snow where the ski tracks were beginning to produce the bumps known as moguls. He turned to me and asked if there was a word for young moguls. I thought for a second and replied 'I'd call them proto-moguls', as you would call an early design a prototype. (*Prótos* is the Greek word for 'first'.)

Which just set me thinking about how much Greek and Latin words are still very much at the heart of our language today. This book is the result of that thought process.

With *Nike, Nurses and Neon*, Nigel Brown has performed a real service for all those who are curious about the English we speak and read today. There are things here to intrigue every reader. I frankly found myself surprised and engaged by derivations on every page. For example, how can I have failed to realise that the Pontefract Cakes in which I delight take their name from a town that was originally called Fractus Pons meaning 'Broken Bridge'?

Everything is presented with a lightness of touch that engagingly includes a fair amount of autobiography. Of course, in a work like this, completeness is impossible and undesirable, but I would welcome Mr Brown's view on the theory that the brand name Hovis is a combination of *homo* and *vis* (Latin for 'man' and 'power'), and allegedly the invention of a schoolboy from Central Grammar School, Manchester.

We are always being confronted with dire warnings about the decline and disappearance of Greek and Latin. This is nothing new; people have been complaining about the crisis in Classics since the middle of the nineteenth century when it was a regular feature in the pages of *Punch* magazine. The discipline of Classics has survived, and will continue to do so, by renewing and reinventing

Foreword

itself. The appearance of this book tells its own story about the ongoing appetite for the Classical past, here shown to be firmly part of our present.

Dr Paul Millett
Collins Fellow in Classics
Downing College
Cambridge

This book has been written for the enjoyment of people who have never had anything to do with Greek or Latin. So no prior knowledge is required.

However, it will be useful at the outset to explain one of the conventions that has been used. As Greek is written in an alphabet that is completely different to the Roman alphabet, the Greek words referred to in this book have been represented in the Roman alphabet that we are all familiar with. For the most part this is very straightforward: *alpha* is 'a', *beta* is 'b', *gamma* is 'g'. However, there are two exceptions because Greek has two versions of the letters 'e' and 'o'.

The letter 'e'

The Greek letter *epsilon* 'ε' is pronounced as in the word 'bet'.

The Greek letter *eta* 'η' is pronounced as in the word 'hair'. In the word definitions *epsilon* is represented by a normal 'e' while *eta* is represented by an accented 'é'.

The letter 'o'

The Greek letter *omicron* 'o' is pronounced as in the word 'hot'.

But before we begin...

The Greek letter *omega* 'ω' is pronounced as in the word 'cold'.

In the word definitions *omicron* is represented by a normal 'o' while *omega* is represented by an accented 'ó'.

CONTENTS
Contents

Contents

Anyone who speaks English is a master or mistress of many languages without realising it. For modern English is not one language, it is many: it is a pot-pourri of French words, a goulash of Hungarian, a cocktail of Middle English, a blend of Old Norse not to mention the hotchpotch of Old French.

In the middle of this great mélange, far and away the greatest influences come from the ancient languages of Greek and Latin. This book delves into the continuing influence that these two languages have in the words we use in our every day conversations. It is an omnibus of Latin, an amalgamation of Greek for everyone everywhere, from the House of Lords to Goodison Park.

It is for the football fan whose replica shirt carries a Latin motto, it is for the shopper in the supermarket buying a tub of Flora, it is for the petrolhead who may be interested to know that Volvo is a Latin word meaning 'I turn'. It has been written for the general reader rather than the academic and is an ideal book to dip into for a few minutes before coming away thinking 'Well I never knew that!'

It's easy speaking Latin and Greek. After all, you've been using both languages all your life.

Whenever you say the word **hippopotamus** you are speaking ancient Greek, the language of Aristotle, Plato and Sophocles. If we want to go native we should call the animal a riverhorse, since hippopotamus is derived from two Greek words – *hippos* = horse and *potamos* = river. Yet we stick with the Greek word because we've been using it for centuries, and if it's not broken don't fix it.

When you talk about your **status** you are using the same Latin word that Cicero, Julius Caesar or the emperor Claudius used to describe exactly the same concept.

And that's just the beginning...

THE MODERN WORLD seems to be obsessed with abbreviations, especially acronyms. Once upon a time we used to talk in sentences, whereas today we often seem to use a series of initial letters. Court cases rely on **DNA** evidence, the **BBC** broadcast **TV** programmes to test the nation's **IQ** and your car needs an **MOT** test. The word **acronym** is derived from two Greek words: *akron* and *onoma* meaning the top of the name.

When it comes to acronyms we could be forgiven for sometimes being confused, but we rarely are. We live in a fast-moving culture where we like to use shorthand, increased by our love of text messaging: ez 4 sum!

Yet some acronyms have become words in their own right because the acronym is easier to say than the words it replaces. **DNA** is a case in point. I bet that if I stood in the market square in Cambridge (one of the world centres of DNA research) and asked a thousand people what DNA stands for I would encounter only a handful who knew the answer. Even if you do know that it stands for DeoxyriboNucleic Acid you're none the wiser, so stick with DNA as a word in its own right.

The fact that the 'A' stands for acid leads me to another acronym: **LSD**. This takes me back to my first days at college and my initial group meeting with my fellow cohorts. Our tutor was explaining to us various of the do's and don'ts of college life. In those days, before mobile phones, he encouraged us to phone home regularly. 'There are three payphones located on staircases D, L and S.' At this point, my mate Duncan piped up, 'or L, S and D if that makes it easier to remember.' These many years later when the payphones have long since been removed, Duncan's comment is the *only* way I can remember where they were. He later claimed that he was referring to the predecimal coinage system of pounds, shillings and pence but we weren't going to buy that one. It more usually stands for LySergic acid Diethylamide. Or Lucy in the Sky with Diamonds. Enough. There are plenty of acronyms and abbreviations that we use today in their pure Latin form. Here are some of the more common ones.

A.D. = Anno Domini – **in the year of our Lord.** We have long been a country of religious diversity but the official calendar remains Christian and years are designated by the number of them that have passed since the birth of Christ.

C. = circa – **about,** used of uncertain dates or quantities.

C.V. = *Curriculum Vitae*, which means the course of your life.

etc. = *et cetera* – **and the rest**. Often used as shorthand by writers who are being lazy creating a sentence such as... there's this thing and that thing and all the rest (that I can't be bothered to enumerate).

M.O. = *Modus Operandi* – **method of working**. Principally heard in T.V. cop dramas to describe the usual way the criminal operates. (Of course, in cop dramas the criminal always commits multiple crimes, so knowing his or her method of working will be helpful in solving murders Two and Three.)

N.B. = *Nota Bene* – **note well**. Used in correspondence to emphasise a particular point. Nowadays, with the benefit of computer technology, we're more likely to emphasise something by typing it in bold type.

P.M. = *Post Mortem* – **after death**.

  = *Post Meridiem* – **after midday**.

Meridiem is a contraction of the Latin *medius dies* meaning **middle day** or 12 o'clock for us.

P.S. = *Post Scriptum* – **after writing**. A postscript is some-thing we add to a document we have finished writing as an afterthought.

q.v. = *quod vide* – **which see**. Used to cross refer to material elsewhere in a piece of writing. Not to be confused with *cf.* which comes from the Latin *confero* meaning **compare**. This is used to suggest that another associated work should be consulted.

viz. = *videlicet* – **that is to say, namely**. The z is not a letter but a sign used to stand for the 'delicet' part of the word in early manuscripts to save space. Why use half an inch of valuable vellum when you don't have to?

What is the difference between?

i.e. *i.e.* (Lat. *id est* = **that is**) used to <u>define the meaning</u> of what has just been said,

... and ...

e.g. e.g. (Lat. *exempli gratia* = **for the sake of example**) used to give an <u>example</u> of what has just been said. So...

If I want a job, I can become a greengrocer
i.e. someone who sells <u>fruit</u>
e.g. <u>apples</u>.

Aqueduct (Lat. *aqua* = water + *ductus* = led)
'You can lead a horse to water but you can't make it drink.'

Most people, and particularly afficianados of Neil Young, will recognise this phrase as a neat way of saying that you can take a negotiation to the brink but you've still got to make the final sale, which is not going to be that easy.

So instead of taking the horse to the watering hole is there any way you can take the watering hole to the horse?

The Romans thought about it and decided that they could. After all, they were the bees', knees when it came to building things. Roads, obviously, but they also had a particular penchant for aqueducts. Why? Because the Romans were obsessed with water. Not simply as a necessity for life, but, as Bill Shankley might have said, because water was much more important than that.

For the Romans water was part of the matrix that held society together. And the place where this happened was the public baths.

These were a little different from the public swimming pools we enjoy today. To the Romans the public baths were an amalgamation of the gym, the pub, the golf club and the brothel all rolled into one.

Aqueduct

First off, they were places where you went to get clean; for the majority of people this was not something you could do easily at home. Beyond that the experience at the baths was something that people did as a social activity, relaxing with friends or doing serious business deals.

The idea of a public bath existed in ancient Greek society and an example has been found with a number of hip baths arranged around the wall of a circular room where people would bathe together in individual tubs.

But it was the Romans who developed the idea of communal pools inside a building open to the general public. It must have been an interesting experience.

Having paid your entrance fee, or in the majority of baths at Rome, having walked in for free, you then embarked on a tour through a series of bathing rooms.

After the changing room your first experience would have been the *frigidarium*, a cold plunge pool. This gives us our word **fridge** (which although it is a shortened form of refrigerator seems to have got closer to the Latin original than refrigerator itself). Another spin off is the word **frigid**, which you would be if you'd just stepped out of a cold plunge pool.

Next stop was the *tepidarium*, a slightly heated warm room designed to help you get your breath back; it gives us the word **tepid**. Finally you would enter the *caldarium*, a room which was strongly heated and contained a pool where the water was probably at a similar temperature to the public swimming pools we are used to today.

The Roman bath-houses were tremendously popular and as they became more sophisticated additional activities were associated with them. Gardens were added, as well as lecture halls, libraries and other facilities such as a gymnasium. This is something we can easily relate to. Modern day fitness centres are often a collection of swimming pool, gym, squash courts and bar.

The difference between the public baths and the **spa** (q.v.) is that the spa had to be situated at the place where the hot spring water rises to the earth's surface. The engineering prowess of the Romans enabled them to site a public bath-house wherever they wanted, thanks to their ability to move water along **aqueducts**.

The finest example that still remains (2000 years or so after it was originally constructed) is the Pont du Gard, which stands just outside Nîmes in Southern France. If you ever get the opportunity to look at it from the valley floor you will see an amazing arrangement of arches on three levels, the topmost of which forms the water course itself.

Aqueduct

It goes from one side of the valley to the other in a perfectly straight line. Except, of course, that it is not absolutely horizontal. It has a very slight incline from one side to the other so that the water can flow. The remarkable skills of Roman surveyors enabled them to create an incline that was virtually imperceptible. For each kilometre of length, the incline would be less than 40 centimetres, or 0.04%. Of equal interest is the word the Romans used for it. Not a water carrier or a water bridge but a water leader. As an ordinary citizen in Rome getting used to the idea that your water is being brought into the city along bridges which seem to be totally horizontal, what would you think? Something (perhaps divine providence) is leading or pulling the water from its far away source into your lap.

However it worked in reality, the idea of providing the public with a constant supply of water was one of the great cultural advances of Roman civilization. The first aqueduct to bring water into Rome was built at the end of the fourth century BC. By the middle of the first century AD Rome was being supplied by nine different aqueducts whose total length was some 420 kilometres. Various estimates have been made as to the amount of water they carried, but it could well have been around half a million cubic metres per day.

The words **Architecture** and **Architect** derive from the Greek word *arkhitekton* = chief builder. In the field of architecture the Greeks and Romans developed fantastic styles, celebrated around the known world, so it is hardly surprising that many of their terms still remain as part of our language today. The first two words in this category, *apex* and *atrium*, are exactly the same words that the Romans used two thousand years ago, although we have given our own slant to their meanings.

Apex (Lat. = the tip of something). The apex is an end where lines converge to a point, such as the top of a spire. The word is also used in medicine to refer to the pointed ends at the bottom of the heart and the lung.

Atrium (Lat. = reception room). The atrium was the central room of a Roman house. The ceiling had an opening through which rain could fall into a central reservoir. In grander houses this reservoir would be a water feature surrounded by columns.

Attic (Gk. *attikos* = of Athens or Attica). In architecture an attic is a small structure right at the top of a building, which was very common in the Attic or Athenian style, hence the word is used today to describe a small room at the top of a house.

Architecture

Capital (Lat. *capitalis* = of the head). The capital is the feature at the top of a column. The word conveys the notion of being at the head of things. This leads to the other uses of capital to represent a big thing: capital letter, capital city etc.

Column (Lat. *columna* = pillar). Columns come in all shapes and sizes. In architectural terms they usually taper towards the top and are used to support the entablature, but some stand alone. Famous examples are Trajan's column in Rome which is beautifully embellished with a spiral frieze depicting Trajan's conquest of the Dacians, and Nelson's column, in London's Trafalgar Square, topped off with its simple statue.

Cornice (Gk. *korónis* = a curved line). A plaster moulding at the junction between ceiling and walls. In strict architectural terms it is a projection at the top of the entablature that helps to keep rainwater away from a building's walls.

Duplex (Lat. = having two folds). An American term for a semi-detached house or double apartment block.

Gazebo A Latin pun. The word coined to mean a structure from which there is a view. The pun stems from the Latin formation of the future tense which ends in ...*bo* e.g. *amabo* = I will love. Hence gazebo, 'I will have a gaze while I sip my G and T.'

Parapet (Gk. *para* = up to, Lat. *pectus* = chest). A low wall at the edge of a roof or the side of a bridge or turret, which protects a person from falling off but allows them easily to see over and shoot off a volley of arrows.

Pilaster (Lat. *pilastrum* = square pillar). A square or rectangular column, particularly one which does not stand alone but forms an integral part of a wall.

Parthenon (Gk. *parthenos* = virgin). One of the best-known examples of Classical architecture, the Parthenon is situated on top of the Athenian **acropolis** (Gk. *akron* = summit + *polis* = city). It is so called because it was dedicated to Athena Parthenos, the goddess Athena, who was always represented as a young woman.

Portico (Lat. *porticus* = arcade). A covered walkway between the side of a building and a row of columns.

Parthenon

Doric, Ionic and **Corinthian** are the three Classical orders of architecture defined principally by the design of the capitals on the columns. Doric is the oldest, providing a simple square stone slab on the top of a simple or fluted column. An Ionic column rests on a compound base and embellishes the capital with two volutes. The Corinthian is the richest in style, its fluted columns having elaborate capitals decorated with acanthus foliage. The different orders are named after three places in Greece: Dóris, Ionia and Corinth.

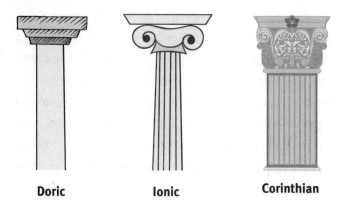

Doric   **Ionic**   **Corinthian**

Astronomy (Gk. *astro* = star, *nemo* = arrange). This is an area of science where the classical languages come to the fore with a big bang. When you compare our technology with what was available to the ancients you have to give them a big hand for what they came up with.

It was my first *Guinness Book of Records* in 1967 that did it for me. The astronomy section definitely has the wow factor. Everything is either so big, so old, or so far away that it's incomprehensible yet fascinating at the same time. Soon afterwards came the Apollo 11 moon landing (we had the afternoon off school to watch some of that) followed by a birthday present of a garden astronomical telescope and late summer evenings learning about the night sky at close quarters. Little did I realise at the time how the knowledge would later provide an interesting topic of conversation when arm in arm with young ladies on late summer evening walks. But I **digress** (Lat. = deviate from the path).

Back to the *Guinness Book of Records*. One entry in particular struck me and stayed with me for years - the date of the next solar eclipse visible from England: 11th August 1999. Not actually my birthday but only three days out. In

1967, as a ten-year-old, 1999 seemed an astronomical age away, but before so long 1999 actually arrived. I met up with friends in northern France for a brief holiday centred around taking in the eclipse. We were well prepared with special viewing equipment and for me an anticipation that had been with me since my childhood. When the vital moment came it was not just overcast, it was raining. Would that dampen our spirits? You bet! Nonetheless, the event was an interesting experience: the sudden darkness, the surprising drop in temperature, the confused birds and plants that began to prepare for nightfall before three minutes later waking up and thinking 'what was all that about?' As for the eclipse itself we had to satisfy ourselves with watching the ongoing TV coverage in our motel rooms. After 32 years of anticipation I saw absolutely nothing of the **eclipse** (Gk. *eklépsis* = failing to appear). You're telling me!

Corona (Lat. = crown). The corona is the circle of light seen around the sun's edge in a total eclipse. By an almost spooky coincidence our moon is exactly the right size to blot out the sun's disc so that at the totality of an eclipse we can see the sun's surface with its solar flares and other emissions. These constantly shifting shafts of hot gases erupting from the surface form an array of spikes, giving the spectacle the appearance of a crown.

Crescent (Lat. *crescens* = growing). The word crescent refers to the waxing or developing moon. It is used as the emblem of the Red Crescent, the Middle Eastern equivalent of the Red Cross. If you ever wondered why crescent has a silent 'c' in the middle, the Latin origin gives you the answer. (The Romans pronounced the 'c' like a 'k', as we did years ago.)

Eccentric (Lat. *ex centrum* = out of the centre). The word was originally applied to the planets since from earth they appear to follow irregular paths. The Greeks and Romans had observed this but had not made the inevitable leap that Nicolaus Copernicus made in the 16th century when he suggested that this effect was caused because the earth was not at the centre of the solar system. And at the time they thought his views were eccentric!

Magnitude (Lat. *magnitudo* = greatness). A word used to describe the luminosity of heavenly objects. Astronomers use a scale whereby the smaller the number the brighter the star. Vega, a prominent star in the constellation of the Lyre, is 0.1, Polaris the pole star is 2.2. The few stars brighter than Vega, such as Sirius, have a negative number.

Nebula (Lat. = mist). A nebula is sometimes a bright area of apparently concentrated stars or a dark area where vast quantities of dust are obscuring the background stars. In both cases the result is pretty misty.

Nova (Lat. = new). A nova is a sudden increase in the brightness of a star, caused by a huge nuclear explosion. One of the most common reasons for this is in a double star system that contains a white dwarf star and an expanding red giant. Hydrogen and helium are drawn from the red giant onto the surface of the white dwarf, starting a nuclear chain reaction. The star appears suddenly to brighten before gradually returning to its former magnitude. This can happen several times to the same star system.

Umbra (Lat. = shadow). The umbra is the area of darkness on the earth caused when the moon blots out the sun's light during an eclipse. (It is a cold, dark and wet place: see the introduction to this chapter.) At the same time, all around the umbra is an area on the earth's surface where the moon is only blotting out a portion of the sun's disc. This area is called the **penumbra** (Lat. *paene* + *umbra* = almost shadow). In the eclipse of 1999 a lot of southern Britain was in the penumbra but only a small area of Cornwall was in the umbra itself.

**Try doing this without
a calculator!**

The Metonic cycle

The moon takes about 28 days
to go through its full phase of
new to full and back again. But 13
lunar months only equals 364 days
whereas our solar year has 365 and
a bit. So the lunar cycle doesn't quite
match the solar cycle. For example, if
there is a new moon on the 2nd January
one year, the equivalent new moon in
the following year will fall on 1st January
and at a slightly earlier time of day.
The phases don't synchronise again
for another 19 solar years. This is
called the Metonic cycle, after the
Athenian astronomer Meton,
who first calculated it in 432
BC. Unfortunately, even
then, there is a slight
time difference. This difference was corrected a century
later by Calippus who stated that after four Metonic cycles,
i.e. 76 years, one day should be omitted.

The cycle is still used today to predict eclipses
and to determine the date of Easter Sunday.

Alpha Centauri

The brighter and more important stars in the night sky are referred to by using a Greek letter and the name of their constellation. So the supergiant Betelgeuse in the constellation Orion is more properly known as Alpha Orionis. Alpha Centauri was made talismanic by Douglas Adams for the small fluffy creatures that came from it but its apparent neighbour **Proxima Centauri** (Lat. *proxima* = nearest) is of more interest to us since it is the closest star to our solar system, being a mere 4.3 light years away.

The ultimate question

Our word **cosmos** is simply a different spelling of the Greek word *kosmos,* meaning order. The Greeks' understanding of the heavens was that everything was in perfect arrangement.

The Romans, on the other hand would have us use the word **universe,** derived from the Latin *universus,* meaning turned into one. Both cultures believed that the gods had a hand in everything so it was natural for them to consider that the heavens had been designed by some ultimate force. We may now have Big Bang and Superstring theories as explanations, but as to how or why Big Bang itself happened have we advanced much in 2000 years? I don't think so.

For practical purposes, cosmos and universe mean the same thing.

The Crab Nebula

A **supernova** (Lat. *super* = above) like a **nova** is a huge explosion, only caused by a different phenomenon.
Stars shine for billions of years but eventually run out of fuel. When this happens the gravitational forces cause an explosion of epic proportions which blows the star apart; for a brief period the star becomes exceptionally bright. The best known example is the Crab Nebula in the constellation of Taurus. This mass of star matter was seen as a very bright object in the sky in July 1054 and was recorded by Chinese astronomers. As it is around 6,000 light years away, the explosion actually happened about 4946 BC.

In the centre is a pulsar: an immensely dense neutron star, just a few kilometres in diameter, which rotates incredibly rapidly – spinning 30 times per second.

What is the difference between a
Supermarket and a Hypermarket?

This is a chicken and egg tale. The **supermarket** really got going in 1930s America and after the war moved across the Atlantic. Before long, the supermarket began to dominate the High Street. As the concept became more popular, supermarkets became the centre of even larger shopping areas with further attachments: boutiques, cafes, entertainment arcades, etc.

The supermarket had evolved into the **hypermarket**. The first one I ever came across was in Ecully, a suburb of Lyons in southern France, where the supermarket was the size of several football pitches. It had masses of attendants on roller blades at the checkouts, going to collect things for customers who had forgotten some vital item on their shopping list and needed someone to go and collect it for them.

But back to the chicken and the egg.

The supermarket came first.

Super is the Latin word for above. So a supermarket is something well superior to an ordinary market. But what do you do when you want a word for something even bigger than a supermarket? Go Greek!

Big shops

Huper is the Greek word for above. Marvellous, call it a hypermarket. Except that the Latin word *super* is itself derived from the earlier Greek word *huper*. So '*huper*' Greek, above became '*super*' Latin, above.

But the Supermarket (Latin) came before the Hypermarket (Greek). So which one is the chicken and which one is the egg? I'll have to think about that one.

Ambrose (Gk.) divine

Andrew (Gk.) manly

Anthony (Lat.) flourishing

Austin (Lat.) grand

Benedict (Lat.) venerated

Cecil (Lat.) poor-sighted

Christopher (Gk.) bearing Christ

Clement (Lat.) mild-tempered

Cornelius (Lat.) horned

Cyril (Gk.) chief

Denis (Gk.) god of wine

Eugene (Gk.) well born

Fabian (Lat.) bean grower

Felix (Lat.) lucky

George (Gk.) farmer

Giles (Gk.) shield

Gregory (Gk.) watchful

Horace (Gk.) guardian

Ignatius (Lat.) ardent

Jocelin (Lat.) just

Julius, Julian (Lat.) soft-haired

Laurence (Lat.) crowned with laurels

Leander (Gk.) lion man

Lionel (Lat.) little lion

Lucius (Lat.) bright

Luke (Gk.) shining

Mark (Lat.) from the god Mars

Martin (Lat.) warlike

Maurice (Lat.) of moorish descent

Nicholas (Gk.) victorious over the people

Nigel (Lat.) black

Oliver (Lat.) olive wreath

Patrick (Lat.) noble

Paul (Lat.) little

Peregrine (Lat.) traveller

Peter (Gk.) rock

Rufus (Lat.) reddish

Stephen (Gk.) crown

Sylvester (Lat.) of woodland

Theodore (Gk.) gift of god

Timothy (Gk.) god fearing

Valentine (Lat.) strong

Victor (Lat.) conqueror

Vincent (Lat.) conquering

Vivian (Lat.) alive

like name, like nature

The name **Philip** is made up of two Greek words, *philos*, 'fond of' and *hippos*, 'horse'. Philip II was king of Macedon in the fourth century BC. He owned racehorses, one of which won a race at the Olympics in 356 BC. He was the father of Alexander the Great.

Alexander, meaning protector of men, is also made up of two words, *alexo*, 'protect' and *andros*, 'man'. Against overwhelming odds Alexander the Great led the men of his army continuously for 13 years as far as the Indian Punjab in the East, Egypt in the south and the Danube in the north.

Brand names

It is hardly surprising that a lot of the brand names we use today link in to the cultural world of the ancient European civilizations. Brand Managers need to foster a feeling of pizzaz that makes their brands look larger than life by association with the heroic and the grandiose.

Or do they just pick a name that sounds good because they've vaguely heard of it before?

I wonder.

Brand	Product	Derivation
Ajax	Dutch football club	Hero in the Trojan War
Ambrosia	rice products	Gk. = food of the gods
Anchor	butter	Lat. *ancora* = anchor
Argos	catalogue retailer	Gk. = shining, bright
Avis	car hire	Lat. = bird
Calor	gas products	Lat. = heat
Flora	margarine	Roman goddess of flowers
Lego	children's toy	Gk. = I arrange in order
Mars	confectionery	Roman god of war
Magnum	ice cream	Lat. = large
Nectar	affinity card	Gk. = drink of the gods
Nike	clothing & footwear	Gk. = victory
Nivea	cosmetics	Lat. = snowy white
Oasis	music band	Gk. = fertile areas of Libyan desert

Brand names

Brand	Product	Derivation
Omega	timepieces	Last letter of Greek alphabet
Saxa	salt	Lat. = rocks
Thermos	drink flask	Gk. = heat
Trident	nuclear subs	Lat. *tridentis* = three-toothed
Triumph	motorcycles	Lat. *triumpho* = I conquer
Vesta	easy-cook meals	Roman goddess of the home
Visa	credit card	Lat. = seen or verified

Cortina (Lat. = cauldron)
A market-leading car in the Sixties and Seventies, the Ford Cortina took its name from the ski-ing resort in the Italian alps, Cortina d'Ampezzo, where it was launched amid extravagant publicity in 1962. The town's name originates from the Latin word for a cauldron since it is situated in an area where the cuisine has a long history of casseroles and stews.

The words we use for the days of the week and the months of the year all go to make up the calendar that we generally have on our desktop, whether electronic or manual. Their origins are a mish-mash of different cultures. The word **calendar** derives from the Latin *kalends* meaning the first day of the month, but only one of the four seasons is Latin, **Autumn** from *autumnus*; spring, summer and winter are all native words. The days of the week are native words except **Saturday**, which comes from *saturni dies*, the day of the Roman god, Saturn. This is largely because the Greeks and Romans didn't use the standard seven-day week that we are used to until it was introduced by the emperor Constantine in AD 321. 'Day', 'month' and 'year' are all native words but **minute** is Latin (*minutus* = lessened) and **hour** is a Greek word, *hóra*. Our months, however, do all derive from Latin.

THE MONTHS OF THE YEAR

January (*januarius mensis* = the month of the god Janus). Janus was the god of entrances and exits, depicted with two faces, one facing forwards and one facing backwards. The Romans were aware that astronomically the beginning of January is around the winter solstice, so Janus looks back to the old year and forward to the new.

The Calendar

February (*februarius*). This comes from the name of a Roman festival of purification held at this time of year. Originally it was a festival of preparation for the administrative new year, which began on March 1st, and for the new planting season. The act of purification was designed to please the gods who would then ensure fertile fields.

March (*martius mensis* = the month of Mars, the god of war). With the bad weather of winter over it was time for the Romans to start waging war again with their neighbours. It was a particularly bad month for the greatest warmonger of them all, Julius Caesar. At the beginning of Shakespeare's play, a soothsayer says to Caesar, 'Beware the Ides of March'. The Ides was the day at the middle of each month falling on either the 13th or the 15th. The Ides of March was the 15th, the day in 44 BC when Caesar was killed on the steps of the senate house. If only he'd stayed in bed he'd have got away with it! Sometimes having a good work ethic can catch you out.

April (*aperio* = open up). The word reflects a general feeling that spring is here and that things are opening up all around us with the first blossom on fruit trees and flowers. It was a time for agricultural festivals.

May (*maius mensis* = the month of the goddess Maia).

Maia was a goddess associated with growth and motherhood since this is a time of natural plant growth.

June (*junius mensis* = the month sacred to the goddess Juno). Juno was the wife of Jupiter and as such was the most important Roman goddess. She was associated with youth, motherhood and fertility in general. June completes a period of three months all named for their association with a time of growth and development in nature.

July (*julius mensis* = the month of Julius) was originally called **Quintilis**, because it was the fifth month after the start of the adminstrative New Year on March 1st. It was later renamed after Julius Caesar.

August. Originally **Sextilis**, the sixth month, it was renamed after *Augustus*, the name which the young Octavius Caesar, great-nephew of Julius, adopted at the end of the civil war when he became the first emperor.

The last four months are the seventh *septem*, eighth *octo*, ninth *novem* and tenth *decem*.

On 31st December 1999 the world counted down to the new **millennium** as the year digits became 2000 (Lat. *mille* = thousand + *annus* = year). Strictly speaking, the new millennium began on 1st January 2001 but the iconic status of the change between 1999 and 2000 seemed far more worthy of celebration.

What is the connection between...?

December and **decimate**?
Both words come from the Latin word for the number ten, *decem*.

December may be our twelfth month but for the Romans it was the tenth. Given that in the UK our tax year starts on 6th April we can hardly critcise the Romans for having an administrative system that didn't start on January 1st.

We use the word **decimate** in a way that a Roman soldier would not quite understand. To us it means to destroy utterly. To him it meant much less destruction but an even more terrifying concept. Decimation was an army punishment given to a group of soldiers that had failed in its task. The cohort in question was divided into groups of ten men who drew lots. The man who drew the short straw then had to be killed by his nine comrades, either by being stoned or clubbed to death. By the second century BC even the Romans thought that the practice was counter-productive and it was outlawed. Decimation was revived in 71 BC by Crassus during the war against the slave revolt led by Spartacus, but then Crassus was a seriously nasty piece of work.

Canopy (Gk. *kanops* = mosquito)

It's not immediately obvious, but canopies and mosquitoes are inextricably linked.

It all goes back to the River Nile.

2,000 years ago Egypt was a province of Rome and was nicknamed the 'grain basket' of the Roman Empire due to the huge amounts of grain it was able to produce and export to Rome whose ever growing population was constantly clamouring for more grain to feed itself. The elite in Egyptian society grew rich on the profits. And when you have a rich elite you have people with more money than they know what to do with. So some entrepreneurs of the time decided to go into the business of providing pleasure cruises on the Nile. (Sounds very much like today, really.)

Most pleasure boats were probably not quite as grandiose as the description in Shakespeare's play, *Anthony and Cleopatra*, where the character Enobarbus describes Cleopatra's Nile riverboat as if it were a water borne palace:

The barge she sat in, like a burnished throne,
Burn'd on the water: the poop was beaten gold

Purple the sails and so perfumed that
The winds were love-sick with them; the oars
were silver...

Cleopatra was in a league of her own, but even for lesser mortals these cruises were the bees' knees. Yet it wasn't so easy cruising up the Nile. After the threat of dehydration your next worst enemy was the ever present mosquito.

A solution had to be found. So in the most expensive riverboat cabins the beds would have lavish curtains draped over them, to protect the travellers at night from biting insects – a canopy in fact.

Mosquito nets may have been around for centuries but I'm still out to get you, canopy or no canopy. No, hang on. I'm the real kanopy.

Car marques

Over the years, some of the most famous manufacturers and models have taken their names from the classical languages. Some of these go back a few years but there are plenty that are still on the road today.

Some prominent manufacturers...

Audi (Lat. = listen). Founded by August Horch in 1910, Audi is a pun on his surname. Horch is an old German word for listen (related to the English word 'hark'). The same derivation gives us the word **audio,** meaning 'I listen'.

Fiat (Lat. = let it be made). The name is actually an acronym of Fabbrica Italiana Automobili Torino, the 'Italian Car Factory of Turin', but you can't help feeling that the words were put in that order deliberately, to create the link with the glory days of the Roman Empire.

Volvo (Lat. = I turn or revolve). Originally Volvo was a brand name for the ball bearings made by the car marque's parent company, SKF.

and plenty of models...

Astra (GM)	Lat. = the stars
Carina (T)	Lat. = a ship's keel or a boat
Clio (Re)	Lat. = muse of history
Corolla (T)	Lat. = coronet
Corona (T)	Lat. = crown

Car marques

Maxi (Ro) from Lat. *maximum* = greatest
Micra (N) Gk. = little
Mini (Ro) from Lat. *minimum* = smallest
Nova (GM) Lat. = new
Octavia (Sk) Lat. = a common Roman girl's name meaning eighth
Viva (GM) Lat. = alive

GM = General Motors, T = Toyota, Re = Renault, Ro = Rover, N = Nissan, Sk = Skoda

...but for sheer quantity, Ford wins hands down...
Focus is the Latin word for the hearth. Sit in front of an open fire and you soon see why we use the word focus as a thing of attention. The **Transit** means 'it goes across'; the old **Zephyr** was named after Zephuros, God of the West Wind; the **Zodiac**, like the astrology chart, is a collection of animals (Gk. *zóion* = animal), and **Orion** was a giant hunter in Greek mythology.

...and three officials

Three of the older Ford names were Prefect, Senator and Consul. **Prefects** (*praefecti*) were a group of Roman officials responsible for the corn supply and the fire brigade, among other things. The **Senators** were the ordinary members of the senate or parliament, while the **Consuls** were the highest elected officers of state. There were two elected each year to preside over the senate's business.

The Christian church in the West has a long relationship with Rome thanks to the conversion to Christianity of the Roman Empire in around AD 312 during the reign of the Emperor Constantine. Yet it is to Greece that we should look for the earliest developments of the Christian movement. The word **Christ**, which was given to Jesus of Nazareth, is a Greek word, *christos*, which means annointed, and it was in Greek not Latin that the earliest versions of the Gospels and other books of the New Testament were written. Our word **church** derives from a Greek word *kuriakos*, which means belonging to the Lord. The word the Greeks used for a church, *ekklesia*, gives us **ecclesiastical,** which covers everything connected with the Church. The Greek word meant to be summoned out, a typical feature of many religions whereby the faithful are summoned out to prayer by bells, gongs or people calling from the rooftops. Early Christian churches were called **basilicas**, another Greek word, which means a king's hall. The word had originally been used to describe an oblong hall, with an apse, situated on one side of the market place and used as law courts and for public assemblies. The **apse** (Gk. *hapsis* = a loop) is a semicircular addition at the east end of a basilica. When used as a law court this was where the principal magistrate's chair was situated. These public halls became exclusively used for religious ceremonies and became ever more grand, leading eventually to the most magnificent form of the basilica, St Peter's in Rome. St Peter's is the most important building in the **Vatican,** which is named after the *Vaticanus Mons*, one of the seven hills of Rome. The Vatican hill got its name from being the headquarters of the *vaticinatores*, Roman soothsayers who professed to be able to foretell events.

Before becoming Christian, the Greeks and Romans worshipped a large number of different gods in **temples** (Lat. *templum* = a consecrated place). This word is seen later in the Knights Templar who protected pilgrims to the Holy Land. The two Inns of Court in London, Inner and Middle Temple, derive their names from being built on the site of The Temple, the headquarters of the Knights.

Inside the church the focus of attention is the **altar** (Lat. *altus* = high). The Romans used an altar which was a consecrated table for making religious sacrifices. It was raised up both to give it importance and so that the people could get a better view of the proceedings. Another focal point of a church is the **font** (Lat. *fontis* = fountain), usually a substantial stone structure which holds water for **baptism**

(Gk. *baptizein* = dip). The structural similarity with a fountain is obvious, but the Latin word also has connotations of being a source of wisdom and thus an association with God's blessing. The central body of the church, called the **nave** (Lat. *navis* = ship) is where the congregation sit. It bears a striking resemblance to an ancient warship with people sitting in rows on either side of the aisle, much like the configuration of a **trireme** (Lat. *triremius* = with three oars), the rowing boat used by both the Greeks and Romans in sea battles, with three rows of oars on each side (Transport q.v.).

If the building is a **cathedral** (Gk. *kathedra* = chair) it is situated within its own **see** (Lat. *sedes* = seat), which refers to the area served by the bishop and represents his seat of authority. The whole area over which the bishop has jurisdiction is his **diocese** (Gk. *dia* + *oikesis* = through administration).

Another word used to describe a building for religious worship is **chapel**. They come in many shapes and sizes, from a single room to the glory of the chapel at King's College in Cambridge. The word chapel comes from the Latin word *capella*, meaning a cape. When St Martin divided his military cloak and gave half of it to a beggar at the gate of Amiens, he wrapped the other half round his shoulders as a cape. This cape was preserved as a relic and accompanied the Frankish kings in war. The special tent which sheltered it became known as the *capella*, and military priests who celebrated Mass in the tent were called *capellani*, from which we get the word **Chaplain**.

Climax (Gk. *klimax* = ladder)

Klimax is the Greek word for a ladder. Which is something you gradually go up to get higher and higher. Until you reach the top. After which point the excitement of the ascent is replaced either by the sheer delight that Rapunzel has been rescued or by smoking a cigarette.

The ladder was a much better idea than trying to use the wig.

Clothing

When I see pictures of models strutting their stuff on the catwalks in the great fashion capitals of the world, my usual reaction is one of **stupefaction** (Lat. *stupefactus* = stunned). The clothing paraded seems to belong to another world – it's certainly not in evidence at the sort of social gatherings I attend. Perhaps I should get out more, or maybe I'm just going to the wrong kind of social gatherings.

The word **fashion** derives from the Latin *factio*, the act of making or doing something (in this case producing outlandish **togs** – see below). The same root also gives us the word **faction**, meaning a clique of people or a closed party. And therein lies the answer. The fashion industry is actually just a specialist faction that holds its own exclusive parties, to which normal people are never invited, hence why very few of us ever see those sorts of clothes on real people. Fair enough. I wouldn't go anyway.

Bib (Lat. *bibere* = drink). You just need to imagine the scene at a real roister of a drinking bout in the decadent surroundings of Imperial Rome where the guests get so paralytic that more wine goes down the front of their tunics than in their mouths. To reduce the problem of stubborn stains, put a piece of cloth around the neck to catch the drips.

The word is used for babies today but as Shakespeare points out, in Jaques' Seven Ages of Man speech, there's precious little difference between a baby and a pissed old fart.

Collar (Lat. *collum* = neck). The collar of a garment simply refers to that part that goes around the neck, anything from a highly starched wing collar to the simple circlet on a T-shirt.

Caligula (early Roman emperor). Caligula was a mad emperor whose name has become a by-word for some of the worst excesses of the Roman empire. His real name was Gaius, 'Caligula' was just a nickname. The son of Germanicus and Agrippina, as a young child he accompanied his father who was campaigining on the Rhine. Dressed up in a miniature army uniform the soldiers named him Caligula which means 'little boot'. He certainly knew how to put the boot in when he grew up.

Designer (Lat. *designare* = designate). The root here is the Latin word *signum*, meaning a sign or mark. The designer is someone who puts his mark on something, which is nowhere more appropriately used than in our love of the designer label.

Diaphanous (Gk. *dia* = through + *phaino* = show). Descriptive of a very light and subtle material so delicate that it is almost transparent. Particularly loved by movie directors using backlighting to reveal the contours of the body (usually female) within.

Fabric (Lat. *fabrico* = make). The Latin derivation means to make a product, hence **fabricate,** and originally comes from the world of metal working. The same sort of process is involved in making any product, including woven material. At its most abstract we use it in phrases like 'the fabric of society'.

Fibre (Lat. *fibra* = filament). A threadlike filament used with others to make a matrix, usually of textile but also of other substances such as glass fibre.

Lace (Lat. *laqueus* = noose or snare). There are two ideas in play here. The Latin *laqueus* is first used to describe a noose in the sense of a circle of string used as a trap to catch animals by the head or by a leg. As the noose tightens, the animal is held fast and this is the sense of laces in shoes. Another sense of the word *laqueus* refers to a net for trapping animals, which is the sense adopted to describe a fabric full of holes.

Material (Lat. *materia* = normal matter). A word used to describe things in the real world. Hence it is a basic substance which is used to create other products, a sense not confined to clothing but strongly associated with it because clothing relates to us all.

Clothing

Panoply (Gk. *pan* = all + *hopla* = weaponry). The word is used to describe a full or splendid array. In medieval times it meant a full suit of armour from its Greek root.

Sandal (Gk. *sandalion* = a little shoe). Something less substantial than a proper shoe, usually a sole with open work on the upper. The Greek word is itself probably of Asiatic origin.

Togs (Lat. *toga*, from *tegere* = to cover). An informal word for our clothes derives from that most formal piece of Roman clothing, the toga, the Roman equivalent to today's business suit. Imagine our own House of Commons filled with people wearing togas rather than suits – not so unsuitable since the behaviour often appears more appropriate to the antics you would expect at a toga party.

Tunic (Lat. *tunica* = T-shirt like garment). The Greeks and Romans didn't quite create the T-shirt, rather more its precursor the tunic – a complete short-sleeved garment belted at the waist and hanging down to the knees. Worn without trousers it was the ideal garment for the heat of the summer.

Uniform (Lat. *uni* = single + *forma* = form). A uniform is something that conforms to a single pattern. In the world of work many people wear uniforms for the recognition of position that it confers.

Velvet (Lat. *villus* = tufty haired). Velvet is a closely woven fabric, originally of silk, with a thick short pile. The Latin word *villus* is variously used for the softness of down or soft hair.

Vest (Lat. *vestis* = garment). The Latin word *vestis* is a general word for any piece of clothing. We have adopted it as a garment covering the upper body because in warm climates covering the legs is less important. The word for clothing in general was *vestimentum*, from which we derive the word **vestment**, referring to a full set of clothes for official or state robes.

...of tars and tents...

Canvas
(Gk. *kannabis* = the hemp plant)

Canvas was originally bleached cloth made from hemp, which proved to be an ideal material for sails and tents since it is very strong and hard-wearing.
Add an extra 's' to canvas and we have the word **canvass** meaning to sound out people's opinions. This word originates from a game which involved tossing a number of dice around in a canvas sheet until only one was left.

The human body is a resilient organism but there are plenty of common complaints that afflict us above and beyond paying taxes. Here are some of them.

Angina (Gk. *agkhoné* = strangling). Angina is a condition which results in chest pain caused by heart and artery disease. When acute it can lead to breathlessness and great distress, not unlike being strangled.

Appendicitis (Lat. *appendix* = addition). The -itis ending is a common one for diseases concerned with inflammation, in this case of the appendix. This strange organ which seems to have no purpose can be fatal if it bursts when inflamed, leading to peritonitis, inflammation of the membrane that stretches around the gut, the **peritoneum** (Gk. *peri* = around + *teinein* = stretch).

Arthritis (Gk. *arthron* = joint). The -itis ending shows that this an inflammatory disease, in this case of the joints.

Asthma (Gk. = gasping). An affliction which causes intense breathing difficulties, sometimes brought on by an allergic reaction.

Bronchitis (Gk. *bronkhos* = windpipe). Bronchitis is another inflammatory disease, this time of the mucous membranes in the lungs. Because coughing is its major symptom the Greeks associated it with the windpipe, although the actual problem is within the lungs.

Diabetes (Gk. *diabainó* = go through). This is a disorder of the pituitary gland such that the body does not absorb sugar and starch, which pass through the body.

Epilepsy (Gk. *epilépsis* = seizure). A nervous disorder which leads to minor or severe convulsions resulting in brief periods of unconsciousness. I suffered a seizure myself in my early forties. According to eye witnesses I suddenly fell to the ground, on my lawn thankfully, and spent five minutes thrashing around and foaming at the mouth, although I was totally unconscious. After numerous medical tests my consultant's report told me that I was perfectly healthy and he could give me no explanation as to why it had happened. The only major consequence was that I had to forfeit my driving licence for a year, during which time I discovered that using public transport, my bike and shanks's pony is a perfectly viable way to live.

Paralysis (Gk. *paralusis* = loosening). Literally a state of complete powerlessness. The effect can be temporary or permanent. The same derivation also gives us **paralytic,** a word which was originally a medical term before being hijacked by medical students to describe themselves on a night out.

Common complaints

Pleurisy (Gk. *pleura* = side of the body). Inflammation of the pleura, the membranes that envelop the lungs. The symptoms are similar to **pneumonia** (Gk. *pneumon* = lung) which is an inflammation of the lungs themselves. So according to everything that has gone before, this should really be called **pneumonitis**.

Rheumatism (Gk. *rheumatismos* = streaming). A disease which leads to inflammation in the joints, muscles and fibrous tissue. The difference between this and arthritis is that rheumatism is an inflammation of the tissue, arthritis of the bone.

Thrombosis (Gk *thrombos* = lump). A coagulation of blood in a vessel or organ which causes a blockage. Its severity will depend on its size and its position in the body.

Ulcer (Lat. *ulceris* related to the Gk. *helkos* = a sore). An open sore which persistently suppurates. It can be external or internal.

Varicose veins (Lat. *varicosus* = with distended veins). Describes surface veins, especially those of the legs, which have become twisted and dilated. We have simply retained in our vocabulary the word used by the Romans to describe the condition.

the effects of seasickness or...
...Nausea (Gk. *naus* = ship)

The Greeks were, and still are, a nation of shipbuilders and seafarers and the Ionian sea can be a hellishly rough place. I know, I've been there. As a student I once took a ten-hour ferry journey from Piraeus to the island of Naxos. The cheapest ticket was Deck Class, which meant you weren't allowed inside the boat except to go to the loo. It was very rough and on the one occasion I did go inside I wished I hadn't, due to the obvious effects of the nausea suffered by the passengers inside. The fresh air of Deck Class was very much appreciated when I got back outside!

The word **constellation** (Lat. *con* = together + *stella* = star) describes a group of stars that form an imaginary outline. In the third century BC a Greek astronomer, Aratos of Soli, mapped out some prominent star groupings and by the Roman era these had been formalised into the constellations we know today. Most were named after animals or figures from Greek **mythology** (Gk. *muthos* = fable + *logos* = story). It is impossible to see the Southern skies from Europe so the southern constellations have been delineated more recently, but still with Latin names.

Some Northern constellations

Aquila – the eagle

Auriga – the charioteer

Bootes – the herdsman

Camelopardalis – the giraffe

Canes Venatici – the hunting dogs

Canis Major – the greater dog

Canis Minor – the lesser dog

The rising of these latter two constellations in Rome was in the middle of July, hence our use of the term 'Dog days' to describe a very hot period.

Corona Borealis – northern crown

Cygnus – the swan

Draco – the dragon

Hercules – he of the 12 labours

Lyra – the lyre

Orion – a famous hunter

Sagitta – the arrow

Ursa Major – the greater bear

Ursa Minor – the lesser bear

Vulpecula – the fox

Constellations

Some Southern constellations

Carina – the keel

Centaurus – the centaur

Columba – the dove

Lepus – the hare

Lupus – the wolf

Musca – the fly

Puppis – the stern

Tucana – the toucan

Volans – the flying fish

(All names are Latin)

Love at first sight...

The Sea Monster

One legend links no fewer than five of the Northern constellations, which all lie next to each other in the sky. **Cepheus** was a king of Ethiopia whose kingdom was being ravaged by a sea monster. In an attempt to appease the monster, Cepheus and his wife **Cassiopeia** chained their daughter, **Andromeda**, to rocks by the shore as an offering. **Perseus** (who just happened to be flying by on his winged horse, **Pegasus**) swooped down, fought and killed the monster, saved Andromeda and married her.

Ever since the Ice Age vanished and people came out of the caves, we have been pretty obsessed with construction. We just love building, as did the Romans before us and the Greeks before them. As society develops so do construction sites. The word **construct** comes from the Latin *constructus* meaning created together, or the result of putting together many different parts into a single entity. This does not only refer to houses, offices and public buildings, but anything that is the end result of lots of things being put together.

Cement (Lat. *caementum* = chipped). A *caementum* was a small piece of stone used as a filling piece in dry stone walls. As cement was developed to do a similar job, it took its name from its predecessor. **Concrete** comes from a Latin word *concretus* meaning thickened, by the addition of small stones into the cement mix.

Edifice (Lat. *aedis* = dwelling + *facere* = make). We tend to use the word edifice to mean something that is permanent rather than temporary, but it really means any dwelling you name, so putting up a tent is still creating an edifice.

Grange (Lat. *granum* = grain). The words grange, *granum* and grain are all very similiar because they are about one of our basics – food. The Latin word *granum* not only gives us grange, the place where grain was stored, but also our granary loaf. It is also responsible for the name of the Granta river from which the city of Cambridge got its original name of Grantybridge, due to its position as a harbour for grain transportation.

Lintel (Lat. *limen* = threshold). The threshold is the front doorway, which has a lintel above, it so the two words have become inter-connected. The word *limen* also gives us **eliminate** (Lat. *eliminare* = to turn out of doors). It is also associated with *limitis,* a boundary, which gives us **limit**.

Manor (Lat. *manere* = stay). This is the place you call your home. People who refer to their home patch as their 'manor' are not wrong. The root word also gives us a number of other words which involve staying around including **remain, remainder** and **remains**.

Marble (Gk. *marmaros* = a rock with sparkling crystals in it). Many of the marbles and granites have impurities in them that give a sparkling effect.

Mortar (Lat. *mortarium* = grinding vessel). The Latin word originally refers to the grinding vessel, which, together with its pestle, we still use in the kitchen today. A larger version was used to prepare the mixture of lime, sand and water, the **mortar,** which took on the name of the vessel in which it was mixed.

Monument (Lat. *monumentum* = a memorial building). A monument does not have to be large but it should always be a memorial of a person or event.

Pavement (Lat. *pavimentum* = beaten). As well as using tiles to make their floors and walkways, the Romans also used stones and bricks which they hammered into place.

Plaster (Gk. *emplastron*). The Greek word means to spread or daub a substance on to an object. So the building term plaster is closely associated with the medical term for a wound application. The medical use comes from the ancient method of dressing a wound, which involved daubing onto a piece of linen an ointment prepared in such a way that it would stick to the skin.

Structure (Lat. *structura* = building). The relationship between the word structure and construction is that the addition of the Latin word *con*, meaning with, gives the idea of putting a whole set of things together, rather than just putting up a single building.

Turret (Lat. *turris* = tower). The basic difference between a turret and a tower is that a turret is a small affair added on to a wall while a tower is usually much larger and can be free-standing. Both words have their origin in the Latin *turris* but **tower** has come to us via the old French word *tur*.

Villa (Lat. = country house). To a Roman this referred not to the ancient football team from Aston but to a house in the country. It may well be connected to the word for a country estate, *vicus*.

Mansion

(Lat. *mansio* = an army tent)

We all know that an Englishman's home is his castle, whether it's a massive pile in the home counties with stables attached or a two-bed flat in Notting Hill. Yet there are some people who just haven't quite understood the idea. (Size is not everything.)

The Latin word *mansio* was a military term for nothing bigger than a tent used on route marches. It later became a word for a roadside inn where soldiers might billet and only much later did it refer to a larger, permanent dwelling. So if someone tries to impress you by talking about the size of their mansion just ask them how long it takes to put it up.

Perhaps we should begin at the beginning.

Not with the chicken but with the egg.

Actually egg is an Old Norse word. The Latin equivalent is **ovum,** which gives us the **ovary** where the eggs are produced and **ovulation,** the process which releases an egg into a female's reproductive system. If it is **fertilised** (Lat. *fertilis* = fruitful) by **sperm** (Gk. *sperma* = seed) then **conception** takes place (Lat. *conceptio* = a taking in). As the fertislised egg enters the **uterus** (Lat. = womb) it becomes an **embryo** (Gk. *enbruon* = swell inside). At this point a woman becomes **pregnant** (Lat. *praegnatus* = produced earlier) and starts going to **antenatal** classes (Lat. *ante* + *natalis* = before birth). In very unfortunate cases a fertilised egg remains outside the uterus and the pregnancy is **ectopic** (Gk. *ek* + *topos* = out of place), a very serious condition.

When the time comes to give birth the **expectant** mother (Lat. *exspectans* = looking forward) may be given an **epidural** injection, for pain relief (Gk. *epi* + *dura* = on something hard), referring to the hard membrane of the spinal cord, but in difficult births a **Caesarian** section may be undertaken, so called because Julius Caesar was supposedly delivered by this method. As the baby is born it is detached from the **umbilical** cord (Lat. *umbilicus* = navel) before being placed in its mother's arms. Some people actually eat the afterbirth or **placenta** (Gk. *plakountos* = flat cake), so named from its shape.

The resulting **infant** (Lat. *infantis* = unable to speak – try telling that to tired parents!) may give some parents **postnatal** depression (Lat. *post* + *natalis* = after birth) but it will gradually develop to **puberty** (Lat. *pubertas* = growth of hair), which is associated with the nether regions (Lat. *os* + *pubis* = pelvic bone).

In **adolescence** (Lat. *adolescens* = growing up) we begin to **mature** (Lat. *maturus* = ripe) and finally become an **adult** (Lat. *adultus* = grown up) at which point we will, in all probability, repeat the whole **process** (Lat. *processus* = a going forward which also, of course, gives us the word **procession**). Eventually we begin to grow old, sometimes becoming **geriatric** (Gk. *géras* = old age + *iatros* = doctor) and even **senile** (Lat. *senilis* = of an old man). Near the end we are said to be **in extremis** (Lat. = in the last parts) and we may be given the last rites.

If we have not died of natural causes the case will be put before the **coroner** (Lat. *corona* = crown) an official of the state. He or she may decide that an **autopsy** (Gk. *autos* + *opsis* = personal sight) or **post mortem** (Lat. = after death) is required. The Latin term is nothing more than a factual description of time while the Greek word conveys a more forensic sense that there should be an eye witness proving no evidence of foul play. By this time **Rigor mortis** (Lat. = stiffness of death) will already have set in. After our **funeral** (Lat. *funerus* = a funeral procession) we may be **cremated** (Lat. *crematum* = burnt) or **interred** (Lat. in *terra* = in the ground) possibly with **eulogies** (Gk. *eu* = well + *logos* = word) but with the definite possibility of having **RIP** on our tombstone (Lat. *Requiescat in Pace* = may he/she rest in peace).

What is the difference between...

...**morality** (Lat. *moralis* = relating to customs) and
mortality (Lat. *mortalis* = relating to death)...?

During our lives we learn about the difference between
right and wrong and formulate our own **moral** code.
We may have high morals or low ones and sometimes need
moral support, but unfortunately we are also **mortal**, which
means that we cannot go on living forever, however morally
good we may have been in this life.

Cures

All cultures from earliest times have had individuals who profess to be able to make ailments better. Whether it is the shaman, the witch doctor or the paramedic, there are numerous people who have the task of **curing** the sick (Lat. *cura* = care).

Better than cure is **prevention** (Lat. *praevenire* = anticipate) and high on the list comes **hygiene** (Gk. *hugieiné* = of health). The Greeks and Romans were aware that hygiene was important to good health without fully understanding what we know today. The Romans were great water engineers, bathed regularly and had sophisticated sewers, all of which made a Roman town significantly more hygienic and therefore healthier than a medieval one.

A pioneer of enlightened practices was Florence Nightingale, a nurse of British soldiers in the Crimean War. Her belief that disease could break out spontaneously in dirty and poorly ventilated environments, while not entirely accurate, did lead to the development of certain practices that improved standards of hygiene.

As well as keeping yourself clean it is also important to keep wounds clean. This is often done by using **antiseptics** (Gk. *anti* = against + *séptikos* = something rotten).

Cures

In 1928, Alexander Fleming discovered **penicillin** (Lat. *penicillum* = paintbrush) – so called because under a microscope it resembles a brush.

Since then a huge number of variants have been developed. This large family of **antibiotics** (Gk. *anti* + *biótikos* = against being fit for life) have almost come to be looked on as the holy grail of cures that will work on anything, or a **panacea** (Gk. *pan* = all + *akos* = cure).

Over the years, particularly in the Victorian era, people have claimed that their patent medicines are miracle cures for all sorts of ills. Any such quack remedy is called a **nostrum** (Lat. = our) referring to the ownership of the idea. In drug trials a control group will be given a **placebo** (Lat. = I will be agreeable), an inactive pill.

Before you can devise a cure you need a **diagnosis** (Gk. *dia* = through + *gnósis* = understanding). This is done by looking at a patient's **symptoms** (Gk. *sumptóma* = event).

...and when you need to go...

A **diuretic** (Gk. *dia* = through + *ouron* = urine) is a substance that makes you urinate more than usual. At the other end of the scale are **laxatives** (Lat. *laxus* = loose) and **enemas** (Gk. *enienai* = send in), usually managed by means of an infusion of warm liquid.

Cures

Some cures aim to make up for deficiences in a patient's body. So people with diabetes who do not produce enough **insulin** need to supplement their own supply. The word insulin derives from the Latin word for an island, *insula*, because the hormone is secreted by cells in the pancreas referred to as the Islets of Langerhans, named after the German anatomist who discovered them.

Dinosaurs (Gk. *deinos* = frightening + *sauros* = lizard) have fascinated children and adults for many years. Their names are almost as interesting as the creatures themselves. It was only during the Victorian age that some people began to speculate on what the animals may have looked like and started to name the different species. Since many skeletons were incomplete, an amount of guesswork was involved and some of the names which we still use today are big misnomers. A good example of this is **stegosaurus**, a dinosaur that had bony plates running the length of its spine. The name derives from the Greek *stego* which means to cover, since the discoverer thought that the plates formed an armour plating that covered the whole body rather than just its back.

Acrocanthasaurus (Gk. *akros* = high + *akantha* = thorn), named for the raised ridge of spines along its back.

Allosaurus (Gk. *allos* = strange), from a misconception that the vertebrae were peculiarly modified. In reality the specimen had simply been crushed.

Ankylosaurus (Gk. *agkylos* = crooked). Alluding to a range of anatomical features in which bones are found fused together.

Dinosaurs

Archaeopterix. (Gk. *arkhaios* = ancient + *pteryx* = wing). An early kind of bird.

Brontosaurus (Gk. *bronté* = thunder). Named for its great size or perhaps from a giant in Greek mythology called Brontes. (Now usually referred to as **apatosaurus**.)

Dromaeosaur (Gk. *dromaios* = swift). A small, lightly built rodent.

Hadrosaurus (Gk. *hadros* = powerful). A huge herbivore.

Megalosaurus (Gk. *megalo* = large). Calculated to have been between 20–25 metres long.

Polacanthus (Gk. *polus* = many + *akantha* = spine). Referring to the spine-like bones that run along the body and tail.

Pterodactyl (Gk. *pteron* = wing + *daktylos* = finger) had a wing supported by a single large finger. It was a true reptile rather than a precursor of the bat.

Sauropods (Gk. *podos* = of the foot). A genera named from the general character of their feet, flat with five toes not unlike those of an elephant.

Torosaurus (Gk. *toreo* = perforate). Its crest is perforated by two large openings.

Triceratops (Gk. *treis* = three + *kerat* = horn + *ops* = face) had two forward-pointing horns on its brow and a nose horn.

Velociraptor (Lat. *velocis* = swift + *raptor* = plunderer). A swift-moving carnivore.

Dinosaur classification was chaotic in the early years and even though there turned out to be some serious errors the original names had become so established that they remained unchanged. One group of dinosaurs were initially named the **phytosaurs** (Gk. *phuton* = plant-eating). Unfortunately, later research showed that they were all **carnivores** (Lat. *carnis* = flesh + *vorare* = devour)!

Some extremes...

Earliest: **Eoraptor** (Gk. *eos* = dawn Lat. *raptor* = plunderer) named in reference to its primitive structure.
Biggest: **Bracchiosaurus** (Gk. *brachion* = arm) had an unusually long upper arm which was longer than the thigh bone. It may have looked something like a giraffe.
Smallest: **Compsognathus** (Gk. *kompsos* = elegant + *gnathos* = jaw). The skull had an elegant, slender elongated jaw.
Fastest: **Tyrannosaurus** (Gk. *tyrannos* = king) named for its size, which when it was named in 1905 reflected the fact that it was the biggest carnivore then discovered.

The early classification of some dinosaurs
turned out to be wrong

Draconian

(Gk. *Draco* = Athenian lawmaker)

So we're no longer allowed to smoke in public places. Thanks be to God say those people who hate the habit with a passion and point to the millions of pounds that smoking-related illnesses cost the NHS. To those who value the right of the individual to make their own rational decisions it is a Draconian law that strikes a blow at personal choice. Hold on a moment? Isn't that a bit strong? It's hardly Draconian, surely.

Draco was an Athenian lawmaker in the 7th century BC who set severe penalties for all crimes. When asked why he advocated the death penalty for even minor misdemeanours, his response was that small offences deserved death as much as large ones because there was no difference. A crime is a crime. So to call a bill that bans smoking in public places Draconian is a bit over the top.

If it was Draconian your punishment would be to die by stoning (or some other ghastly exit). Actually, if you are caught smoking today, it's just a fine. So not Draconian at all. Unless the law has a hidden clause for stoning (or other ghastly exit) of which we have not been made aware...

Human beings have been experimenting with substances for centuries and have both used and abused them. Although the abuse of drugs is a worldwide problem it should not be forgotten that there are many, both **synthetic** (Gk. *suntheitkos* = put together) and **natural** (Lat. *naturalis* = produced by birth) that have immense curative use. The debate continues about whether **cannabis** should be legal or not. The Greek *kannabis* was the word for the hemp plant and although the Greeks knew about drugs it is unlikely that they used cannabis to get high. There is a reference to drug taking in Homer's epic, *The Odyssey*, where a woman is described 'casting a drug into the wine'. The link with wine is not surprising since, for the Greeks, wine was the drug of choice, although there is some evidence that other drugs were taken in association with religious practice and oracles. One of these may have been a form of **codeine** from the Greek word *kódeia* or poppy head. **Codeine** is an alkaloid taken from opium and used as an **hypnotic** drug (Gk. *hupnos* = sleep). It can also be used as an **analgesic** (Gk. *analgésia* = lack of feeling).

One of the more modern drugs, **ecstasy**, derives from the Greek word *ekstasis* meaning to put oneself out of one's senses. This is a fairly good description of all **narcotic** drugs

Drugs

(Gk. *narkotikos* = grown numb), when your senses may become heightened but your ability to react to the real world is significantly reduced. The Greeks certainly knew about **opium** (Gk. *opion* = poppy juice). Prepared from the opium poppy, it is smoked or eaten as a stimulant or **intoxicant** (Gk. *toxikon* = arrow poison). It was used years ago as a sedative when it was referred to as **laudanum**, a name given to it in the 16th century by the Rennaisance scientist, Paracelsus. He considered that its medicinal properties were so useful that he coined the name from the Latin word *laudare*, to praise.

The word **addict** derives from the Latin *addictum*, which means surrendered or having given oneself up as a slave, which is what happens to people who take the most powerful drugs.

...and here's a surprise...

Used as we are to all things medical being derived from Greek and Latin, some of the more common words in this category are not. Alcohol is Arabic, Barbiturate was named after a woman called Barbara, Cocaine is Spanish, Heroin is German and Nicotine is French (named after a French diplomat, Nicot, who introduced tobacco to France in the 16th century).

Education

Education comes from the Latin word *educare* meaning to rear. This in turn is closely connected with *educere*, meaning to lead or draw out. To some, education may well seem to be a drawn-out process which they wish to end as soon as possible. To others, education is something so drawn out that it lasts a lifetime. This is closer to the sense of the Latin meaning, which is about taking a person out into the world to gain new experiences from which they learn. The words included in this section have a very academic feel about them; this is not unconnected with the fact that for centuries Greek and Latin formed the bedrock of educational establishments across Europe.

Right up until the 1960s you could not gain admission to an Oxbridge college to read any subject at all unless you had an 'O' level in Latin. Times have changed, yet the words featured here will still be familiar to many.

A good starting point is to look at the word **academic**. The word's origins go back to the Greek philosopher Plato. He was quite a cool dude, who taught his pupils in his garden sitting below a statue of the god *Akadémos*. Plato's reputation was immense and people flocked to hear him. As far as celebrities went back then, he was the Beckham of his day. (Possibly slightly more philosophical in his thinking, mind.) So the place where he spouted his life-enhancing utterances became known as the Academy, by association with the statue of the presiding god.

The word has, of course, been hijacked by the organisation that each year awards the Oscars but I suspect their statue is a very poor imitation of the original.

Alma Mater (Lat. = bounteous mother). A title used by former pupils for their schools, colleges and universities. If you have a good time in education, it's a bounteous place because you get a bonus from it in later life.

Alumnus (Lat. = a nursling or foster-child). A former pupil who has been nurtured by the academic institution in question.

Aegrotat (Lat. = he is sick). A certificate given by a college or university saying that the student is too sick to attend an examination but has been given a pass anyway.

Cave (Lat. = beware). In public schools the word *cave* or KV has long been used as a code word to mean 'watch out a Master is approaching'. It also gives us the word *caveat* meaning a reservation or something to beware of.

Campus (Lat. = field). The area that encompasses all the buildings of a University. The Latin word properly means any level surface especially one used for military training.

So a University area that has no green fields and loads of concrete can still be a campus.

College (Lat. *collegium* = partnership). The collegiate universities developed in the Middle Ages through like-minded people coming together in a group or partnership. It was only when those groups decided to have buildings that the word transferred to the buildings rather than the group.

Didactic (Gk. *didaktikos* = of teaching). Something didactic is designed to instruct.

Diploma (Gk. = folded paper). Diplomas used to be written on parchment, folded and sealed. So if you have any kind of diploma, however hard you have worked for it, at the end of the day you just have a piece of folded paper.

Erudite (Lat. *eruditus* = trained). The Latin word *rudis* means untrained and leads us to the various meanings of **rude**: vulgar or basic. This is also the basis of rudimentary. The Latin prefix *e* is short for *ex* meaning out of. So someone who is erudite has been taken out of the untrained area and has thus become the opposite: highly trained.

Emeritus (Lat. = earned). An emeritus professor is one who has been discharged from service but who still holds an honorary title and may well continue in some other academic capacity.

Exeat (Lat. = he or she may go out). Exeats have their grounding in boarding schools where children are confined to the school campus for the whole term. Save when an uncle or aunt might be passing and would like to meet up with the child for afternoon tea (or a lunchtime pint), at which point an *exeat* could be sought.

In loco parentis (Lat. = in the place of a parent). Particularly in universities and colleges there is usually some kind of tutor given the task of looking after the general well-being of a student away from home. Many students can't wait to get away from their parents but it's always handy to have someone to fall back on.

Matriculate (Lat. *matricula* = a register). This simply means to admit as a member of a University. *Matricula* is the diminutive of **matrix**, which is Latin for womb, the place where things develop. So the day of your matriculation marks the beginning of your academic development.

Mentor. Not too far removed from whoever is *in loco parentis*, a mentor is a wise guide. Mentor was a friend of Odysseus, he of the Wooden Horse fame at the end of the Trojan War.

Pedagogue (Gk. *paidos* = boy + *agein* = lead). The word is generally used to mean a schoolteacher but in ancient

Greece had a more specific usage to describe a slave who accompanied his master's son whenever he left home.

Peripatetic (Gk. *peri* = around + *patein* = walk). Itinerant. Going about one's business from place to place. The term originally related to the Greek philosopher Aristotle who had a habit of walking around in his school, the Lyceum, while teaching.

Quadrangle (Lat. *quad* = four + *angulus* = angle). A quadrangle or quad can be any four-sided geometric figure but is usually used to refer to the enclosed courtyards in Oxford colleges. The same areas in Cambridge colleges are called Courts.

Regius (Lat. *regis* = leisure). The word originally related to conversations during periods of leisure and the knowledge gained from them. Eventually it came to mean the place where such knowledge was taught.

School (Gk. *skholé* = leisure). The word originally related to conversations during periods of leisure and the knowledge gained from them. Eventually it came to mean the place where such knowledge was taught.

University (Lat. *universitas literarum* = entire scope of literature). Medieval universities were places where a student went to learn many subjects, not the specialisation we have today. Students began with the *Trivium* (Lat. = a place where three roads meet) the three roads in question consisting of Grammar, Logic and Rhetoric. This was followed by the *Quadrivium* (Lat. = four roads) of Arithmetic, Astronomy, Geometry and Music.

The words **trivial** and **trivia** derive from the idea that the *Trivium* was the beginner's course about the basics and by association, the simple or trivial.

Viva voce (Lat. = with the living voice). A *viva* is an oral exam where the student is interviewed directly by his examiner. (So no chance of cheating.)

Learning in church...

In pre-reformation England the **primer** (Lat. *primus* = first) was used as a name for the prayer book. This was in many cases the first book that a child had ever seen and was their first reading book. This sense continued, and so gradually primer came to mean the first book you use in a new study. The prayer book is also responsible for the word **rubric** (Lat. *rubrica* = red ochre). The titles and instructions in the prayer book were, and still are, printed in red type, hence our modern usage of rubric as explanatory words.

The ancients were aware of chemical properties and understood that there were elementary substances in nature. Indeed, the Romans used the word *elementum* to mean something like 'the beginnings of other things'. The majority of the names we use for elements today have been created over the last few hundred years from Greek and Latin words that reflect the property of the newly discovered element, e.g. **radium** (Lat. *radius* = ray) because it is a substance that emits powerful radiation.

Elements where the symbol relates to the Latin word for it

Gold	Au	*aureum*	**Iron**	Fe	*ferrum*
Lead	Pb	*plumbum*	**Silver**	Ag	*argentum*
Sodium	Na	*natrium*	**Tin**	Sn	*stannum*

Elements named after associated words

Arsenic	As	Gk. *arsenikos* = yellow dye
Bromine	Br	Gk. *brómos* = stink
Cadmium	Cd	Gk. *kadmeia* from Cadmus, founder of Thebes where it was abundant.
Calcium	Ca	Lat. *calx* = lime
Carbon	C	Lat. *carbonis* = of charcoal
Chlorine	Cl	Gk. *khlóros* = green

Elements

Chromium Cr   Gk. *khróma* = colour – its compounds are very colourful

Copper Cu   Lat. *cyprium* (*aes*) = Cyprus (metal)

Iodine I   Gk. *iódés* = violet-like

Magnesium Mg   Gk. *magnesia* (*lithos*) = (stone) from Magnesia in Turkey

Silicon Si   Lat. *silicis* = of flint

Sulphur S   Lat. *sulfur* = lightning

Elements with amusing derivations

Argon A   Gk. *argon* = idle

Gallium Ga   Lat. *gallus* = cockerel. Translation of Lecoq de Boisbaudran who discovered it.

Neon Ne   Gk. *neon* = a new thing

Rhodium Rh   Gk. *rhodon* = rose, because of the colour of its compounds.

Xenon Xe   Gk. *xenon* = a strange thing

The Sun's Fuel

The sun is principally made up of **hydrogen** (Gk. *hudro* = water + *gen* = producing), which is gradually being converted into **helium** (Gk. *helios* = sun). Worryingly, when all the fuel is used up, the sun will expand before it blows up. Luckily, this will not happen for another several billion years.

Entertainment is a wide-ranging area, covering the performing arts, the venues we go to and some of the performers themselves.

Ars Gratia Artis (Lat. = art for the sake of art). The motto of Metro Goldwyn Mayer means that you can create art for its own sake, the money is peripheral. The band 10CC put it better: 'art for art's sake, money for God's sake.'

C.D. (Lat. *compactus* = confined + Gk. *diskos* = discus). CDs may be pretty modern but their full title of compact disc is a very apposite one. Disc is a short form for discus and *compactus* means both put together and confined. So you could say that your favourite 'Best of' album on compact disc has had all the tracks put together and confined on a little discus.

Carnival (Lat. *carnis* = flesh + *levare* = put away). Carnival was a fiesta in medieval times that paved the way for Lent. In other words, you are coming up to a period of fasting when you put all meat away from the dining table. Of course during the run-up you can put away as much as you like. If you have ever been to Carnival in Brazil you'll realise that they have a completely different idea about what putting away meat means.

Choreograph (Gk. *khoreia* = dancing to music + *graphó* = write down). A choreographer, who writes down the moves in a ballet or other dance sequence, is to ballet what a playwrite is to drama.

Chorus (Gk. *khoros* = a dance in a ring). Originally in Greek drama the dancers in the chorus were the principal attraction. Gradually the actors took on more and more prominence until at the height of the art the chorus had developed into a singing and dancing backdrop to the main action.

Circus (Lat. = ring). The most famous use of the word circus is in the phrase '*panem et circenses*' or 'bread and circuses'. This was coined by the first century Roman satirist, Juvenal, to attack those politicians who doled out free bread and put on lavish events at the circus in an attempt to gain power through overt populism. The circus in Rome was the equivalent of a football stadium today. It provided an afternoon out where you got your passions up, ate rubbish pies in the interval and went home either elated or miserable.

Dido (Lat. = mythical queen of Carthage). During the summer of 2004 the popular singer Dido had a number one hit with 'The White Flag' in which she promised to 'go down with this ship'. Her predecessor, Dido the Queen of Carthage, figures as a star in Virgil's epic, *The Aeneid*, when she delays Aeneas on his travels to found Italy. After protracted dealings she also goes down with her ship (speaking metaphorically).

Episode (Gk. *epeisodion* = an entry). An episode is a small part of a grander theme. We tend to use the word to describe one TV programme in a series. The Greek derivation relates to a way into something and in this context a passage which introduces a new subject into the play.

Fair (Lat. *feria* = holiday). The link between a fair and a holiday is steeped in the consciousness of most European cultures. The link to the fairground is obvious in the sense that fairs come to town when it is holiday and there will be people about. The Latin word is the same in Italian today. In August in Italy you will often see a business sign saying '*chiuso per ferie*', closed for the holidays. So basically, they're all at the coconut shy.

Gladiator (Lat. *gladius* = short sword). Gladiatorial combat was entertaining to the spectators but brutal for the participants. In a non-league contest you might take a lot of flesh wounds but if you were in a bout at the Colosseum it would have been a life and death struggle, literally. Your average gladiator fought with the *gladius*, a short stabbing sword which was the stock item of a Roman infantryman, but for additional fun he would be set against a different kind of fighter such as the retiarius who had a weighted net to ensnare his opponent.

Hippodrome (Gk. *hippos* = horse + *dromos* = course). The name of the course for chariot races as seen, for example, in the film *Ben Hur*. The name became very popular for provincial theatres across the UK in the Edwardian era.

Lyceum (Gk. *lukeios* = a name of the Greek god Apollo). The Greek philosopher, Aristotle, taught his followers in a garden called the Lyceum. It took its name from a neighbouring temple dedicated to Apollo.

Odeon (Gk. *oideion*). The *oideion* was a public building at Athens built by Pericles for musical performances although it was more often used as a law court. It has long been a common name for cinemas in the UK.

Ovation (Lat. *ovatio* = exultation). An ovation is an outburst of often spontaneous applause, sometimes accompanied by standing. In Rome it was a lesser form of a Triumph, the ceremonial procession of a successful returning army commander.

Palladium (Gk. *Pallas* = another name for the goddess Athena). The Palladium was a wooden statue of the goddess Athena, usually referred to as Pallas Athena. The statue is attested to have been in one of the temples of

Rome and thus associated with an important building, hence a grand theatre.

Person (Lat. *persona* = actor's mask). In drama, Greek and Roman actors wore masks to indicate who they were playing.

Phonograph (Gk. *phóné* = sound + *graphó* = write). An early recording device which etched the sounds on to cylinders. It was superseded by **gramophone**, a word formed by reversing the constituent parts of **phonogram** (Gk. *phóné* + *gramma* = a sound written down).

Proscenium (Gk. *pro* = in front of + *skénion* = stage). The part of the stage in front of the curtain line, particularly applied to the arch behind which the curtain is fixed.

Status Quo (Lat. = position in which). This means the unchanged position. After several decades and still going strong, the band of the same name is very much in an unchanged position.

Symphony (Gk. *sumphónos* = agreeing in sound, harmonious). A symphony is an elaborate musical work which brings together many sounds into a harmonious whole.

Thespian A word for an actor, its origin is in Thespis, a Greek poet of the 6th century BC who is one of the first people specifically recorded as being connected with Greek Tragedy plays.

Trilogy (Gk. *trilogia* = three words). A trilogy was a group of three interconnected tragedies to be performed in succession. The Greeks were partial to poetic contests where dramatists had to present a full trilogy plus a satiric drama in a single day.

Volume (Lat. *volutus* = rolled up). Books were originally written on long rolls of parchment attached to a wooden roller at each end, so that they could be wound up for easy storage.

Films with classical titles:

Arachnophobia starring Jeff Daniels came out in 1990. It's title is the Greek for fear of spiders.

Equus, (1977) starring Peter Firth and Richard Burton is the Latin word for a horse. It is a psychological drama that mirrors the demons of a disturbed stable-lad and his psychiatrist.

Gladiator the Ridley Scott film, was released in 2000. Starring Russell Crowe, it won five oscars.

There are several versions of **Quo Vadis**, much the most famous of which was made in 1951 and starred Peter Ustinov. It is a Latin phrase that means 'where are you going?'

The 1976 film, The **Omen**, starred Gregory Peck and Lee Remick. *Omen* is the Latin word for a sign.

The Greek prefix *téle* means **far** and is used in lots of familiar English words...

Our **television** sets are never far away, but the word means 'seeing from afar' because the events we watch are coming to us from a distance away. The further the better in the case of the **telethon**, a word coined from the *tele* part of television and the *thon* of marathon.

Of more use is **teletext**, a word made up in much the same way as telethon, to mean viewing text on the telly.

As ubiquitous as the television is, so is the **telephone** (Gk. *phóné* = sound) where it is the sound that is coming from afar. It is the phone that gives companies the means to do **telemarketing** and **telesales**.

Accustomed as we are to text and e-mail, the international **telex** network which uses **teleprinters** is still a popular system for business. Telex is a contraction of **Tel**egraph and **Ex**change, which brings us to **telegraph**, meaning writing from afar; highly appropriate if you are a foreign correspondent for the national newspaper of the same name. **Telegraphy** involves the transmission of messages without pieces of paper changing hands. Originally this referred to operators using Morse Code devices but there is no reason not to use the word to cover modern electronic media, fax etc.

Far-reaching

Before computers became widespread people could use the Post Office network to send **telegrams**, *gramma* being Greek for a letter. And all of this is classed as **telecommunications**.

The **telescope** enables you to see from afar (Gk. *skopos* = look). So what, you may ask, is the difference between that and a television? The first to be invented was the telescope, which was named after two Greek words meaning sight from afar. When TV was invented a different solution was needed. At some point someone had the bright idea of adding an English word instead, vision, which is itself derived from the Latin word *video*, I see.

Keen photographers have **telephoto** lenses to capture light from afar (Gk. *phótos* = light).

In the field of the **paranormal** (Gk. *para* = beyond + Lat. *norma* = a carpenter's square, hence accurate) some people claim to be **telepathic** (Gk. *pathos* = experience) and others the ability to perform **telekinesis** (Gk. *kinésis* = motion) or movement from afar, whereby, using nothing more than the power of thought they can **teleport** (Lat. *portare* = carry) objects from one place to another.

Personally I'm **sceptical** (Gk. *skepsis* = examined). I've examined the idea and I think it's tosh.

As an increasingly secular and diverse society, the various festivals and services of the Christian Church may not be as well known as they once were but they still have plenty of resonance.

Advent (Lat. *adventus* = approach). Advent covers the season before Christmas. Ever since the Advent Calendar became widespread it has generally been accepted that Advent begins on December 1st and finishes on Christmas Eve. The first record of an Advent calendar is in 1851. It was also popular to burn Advent candles on each day leading up to Christmas.

Ceremony (Lat. *caerimonia* = religious worship). The Latin word relates specifically to religion but we now use it to describe non-religious events as well.

Corpus Christi (Lat. = the body of Christ). A service that is held on the Thursday after Trinity Sunday. It is also the name of colleges at both Oxford and Cambridge.

Epiphany (Gk. *epiphaneia* = showing off). Epiphany covers the twelve days of Christmas (itself an Old English word for the Mass of Christ). The idea of showing off refers to the period when Christ was first revealed to the Magi and others.

Requiem (Lat. = repose). A special Mass to pray for the peace in death of the departed. Mass itself comes from the Latin *missa*, sent, as in send-off, or the nearest you can get in Church to a bit of a party.

Rogation (Lat. *rogatio* = asking). The litany of the saints chanted on the Monday, Tuesday and Wednesday between Rogation Sunday and Ascension Day. The word Litany comes from the Greek *litaneia*, meaning prayer.

Sacrament (Lat. *sacramentum* = solemn oath). The sacrament is a religious ceremony which uses an open act to demonstrate a spiritual commitment.

Nones (Lat. *nonus* = ninth)

Lovers of the *Brother Cadfael* novels will be used to the day of the medieval monastery being punctuated by its various prayer times. These are named using the **ordinal** numbers with the day starting at 6.00am. (Ordinal comes from Latin *ordinis* of a series. First, second, third etc. define a position in a series.) **Prime** is the first office (Lat. *primus* = first). The **nones** is the ninth hour which ends at 3.00pm. So just in time for traditional kick-off on a Saturday.

Food and drink

Hollywood has often portrayed the Roman dining room as a place full of fat gluttons gorging themselves on huge banquets. Before you dismiss this out of hand you should read 'Trimalchio's Dinner', part of the Satyricon written by Petronius, a minister of the emperor Nero. It is a description of the feast of a hundred dishes with everything from thrush starters to wild boar cooked with acorns. If you prefer something knocked up using ingredients available in your local supermarket you can follow a number of original recipes by a 4th century AD **cook** (Lat. *coquus*) called Apicius.

The Roman word for the kitchen, *culina*, is the basis for all things **culinary**. Any self-respecting *culina* would also have a separate room called the *laridum* specifically for keeping cured meat, although we now use the word **larder** for any food storeroom. I have encountered the modern equivalent of a *laridum* in Italy.

In 1987 my brother, his wife and I bought a farmhouse in Umbria. As we went through the years of doing it up I made friends with a local farmer, a larger than life character called Pilo (his schoolday nickname derived from the Latin word for a javelin, *pilum*). Like all Italians he found it difficult to pronounce my first name so he called me Neegel. This I could cope with. More difficult to cope with was a session in Pilo's *laridum*.

Pilo had a commercial vineyard and sold most of his grapes to the local co-operative but saved some to make enough wine to last himself a year. In Pilo's case this was stored in two huge half barrels in his wine cellar, one white, one rosé (whenever he spoke this revered word he put a heavy accent on the é and twirled his hand with a flourish). The white was only marginally preferable to petrol but the rosé was quite quaffable. The only drawback was that he served it in large tumblers, at least three per visit and I had to drive back across the valley and up the other side on a decidedly dodgy hillside road. Its attraction was the delightful odour that met you as you entered Pilo's wine cellar since the old oak barrels with their contents of wine were not the only inhabitants. Hanging from the ceiling must have been twenty curing hams and double that quantity of home-made salamis. The atmosphere was mouthwateringly musty. We did try one of Pilo's salamis once, thinking it would be a succulent antipasto to our evening meal. However, after we had blunted one knife trying to cut through it we decided to hang it from one of the kitchen beams as a rustic ornament.

So, whatever your pretentions to having a larder in your home, remember that it's good to have some wine in it it but it is absolutely essential for authenticity to have some cured meat hanging from the ceiling!

Beaker (Gk. *bikos* = an earthen wine vessel). Originally a *bikos* was a large wine vessel but gradually the word came to mean something the size of a  cup. Beaker People is a term used to describe a Bronze Age people in whose graves pottery beakers are often found.

Benedictine. An old order of monks known originally for their academic skills and now almost exclusively for the liqueur made in their name. The bottles still carry the mark D.O.M. which stands for the Latin motto '*deo optimo maximo*' meaning 'to the finest and greatest god' – so, Bacchus then (Roman god of wine).

Biscuit (Lat. *bis* = twice + *coctum* = cooked). Originally the word used for a cracker, as in ship's biscuit. They were cooked twice to make them hard and long-lasting for sea voyages. The word biscuit is also applied to pottery that has been fired but not yet glazed i.e. cooked twice.

Cereal (Lat. *Ceres* = the goddess of agriculture). The Greeks and Romans cultivated wheat, barley, oats, rye and millet. Wheat became the favoured crop because it contains more gluten which raises loaves during baking. The goddess Ceres had a daughter, Proserpina, who was kidnapped and taken to the underworld by her father who would only release her to be with her mother for six months of the year. This myth, which appears in many cultures, refers to the natural growing season for cereal crops during the summer months.

Colander (Lat. *colare* = to strain). A simple device that is as old as the hills. Colanders have been found in excavations from Pompeii to Scotland, alongside saucepans, pots and other utensils which 2,000 years on remain virtually unchanged in appearance.

Currant. A corruption of Corinth, the town in mainland Greece from where the currant originated.

Claret (Lat. *claratum* = made clear). The word was originally used to describe wines which are light-red in colour.

Epicurean. The Greek philosopher Epicurus held that the highest good was life itself and the aim of life was pleasure or absence of hurt. Wise people refrained from those activities which could later give them pain. So a huge plate of steak, chips and all the trimmings washed down with two bottles of claret was not really the sort of thing he was advocating.

Food and drink

Faggot (Lat. *ficatum* = fed on figs). As the French force feed geese to fatten the liver so the Romans did the same with pigs by fattening them on figs (*ficae*).

Farrago Today we use the word to describe any kind of miscellaneous collection, but the Latin word *farrago* specifically referred to a mixture made up to produce cattle meal.

Fork (Lat. *furca* = fork). The Roman furca was a two pronged item used in agriculture like a pitchfork. In the dining room, where the Romans fed themselves with their fingers, the only piece of cutlery you would find would be a knife.

Margarine (Gk. *margaron* = a pearl). So called because the first developers of the product thought it looked like margarite, a pearl-like mineral.

Mint (Gk. *mintha*). The king of herbs, mint has always been attractive to humans because of its sweetness. The Greek derivation also gives us the word **menthol**.

Nectarine (Gk. *nektar* = divine drink). Nectar was the drink of the Olympian gods, the finest tasting liquid you could find. So if you don't like nectarines you should avoid any invitations to dine up at Mount Olympus.

Pontefract Cakes. The name Pontefract first appears in 1097 when a fellow called Orderic called the place *Fractus Pons* (Lat. = broken bridge). This became *Pontefractus* some time later. It is an allusion to a bridge over the River Aire which had been broken by William the Conqueror in 1069. These sweets, the size of a 50 pence piece, are lovely if you like liquorice.

Semolina. Semolina is made from grains left after the milling of flower and it is used to make puddings and forms of pasta. The derivation is the Latin word for flour, *semila*. This in turn is related to the Latin word *mola,* a grindstone, from which our word **mill** derives.

Sauce. The origin of the word sauce is the Latin *salsus* which means salted. An amount of salt is necessary for all mammals and sauces form an important way of adding extra flavour and nutrients to basic foodstuffs.

Simnel cakes. (Lat. *siminellus* = fine bread). Rich cakes formerly eaten (especially in Lancashire) on Mothering Sunday, Easter and Christmas.

Thermidor. Lobster Thermidor has always had the reputation of being an extravagant dish. Its name comes from two Greek words, *thermé*, heat, and *dóron*, gift. Clearly the gift of heat was taken more literally by the French Revolutionaries when they decided to completely rename their calendar. For them Thermidor was the 11th month and it began on 19th July. That's revolutionaries for you.

Venison (Lat. *venatio* = hunting). Today venison strictly applies to deer meat but the Romans used it to refer to any food gained from hunting.

What is the difference between?

...voracious (Lat. *voracis* = greedy) and **veracious** (Lat. *veracis* = truthful).

If you have a pub meal consisting of a starter, a main course, a dessert and a helping from the cheese board, you may well consider yourself to have a **voracious** appetite. If you are sitting with a companion who is **veracious** you may well be called a greedy pig.

Good wine needs no bush

Got a great product? Then advertise it and sell it! But before you do, you need an icon like a great big roadside M for hamburgers or... an ivy bush for wine? Oh, yes. If you were a publican in the Roman world it was customary to advertise your establishment by having an ivy bush outside. Indeed, you will still come across pubs in the UK called the Ivy Bush. Of course, in all retailing you get a certain snob value from the establishments who say 'our product is so good we don't need to advertise, it sells itself'. Which led to the Latin proverb *vino vendibili hedera non opus est* or 'where the wine is saleable there is no need of ivy'.

A better known Latin motto is *in vino veritas*, which means 'in wine the truth', or 'have one too many and there is no knowing what you might say'. (Or do, for that matter.)

There is quite a crop of football clubs sporting Latin mottoes. It is up to the reader to decide whether or not the mottoes are appropriate to each club. The high moral values of virtue, industry and hard work reveal a Golden Age of motto writing in Victorian times. Quite what the founders of Newport County had in mind remains a mystery. Sadly, it is impossible to include Aston Villa in this list as the club's motto 'Prepared' is not Latin.

Arsenal – *Victoria concordia crescit* Victory grows with harmony

Blackburn Rovers – *Arte et labore* With skill and hard work

Bournemouth – *Pulchritudo et salubritas* Beauty and healthiness

Bristol Rovers – *Virtute et industria* With virtue and industry

Bury – *Vincit omnia industria* Industry conquers everything

Carlisle United – *Unita fortior* Stronger by being united

Crewe Alexandra – *Semper contendo* I always strive

Everton – *Nil satis nisi optimum* It is not enough unless it is the best

Fulham – *Pro civibus et civitate* For the citizens and the state

Luton Town – *Scientiae et labori detur* To knowledge and hard work

Mansfield Town – *Sicut industria quercus virescit* As the oak flourishes by hard work

Newcastle United – *Fortitor defendit triumphans* Let the triumphant defend bravely

Newport County – *Terra marique* On land and sea

Football club mottoes

Oldham Athletic – *Sapere aude* Dare to be wise

Reading – *A deo et regina (Victoria)* By God and the Queen (Victoria)

Rochdale – *Crede signo* Believe in the badge

Rotherham – *Sic virescit industria* Thus it flourishes by industry

Sheffield Wednesday – *Consilio et animis* With prudence and with passion

Shrewsbury Town – *Floreat salopia* May Shropshire flourish

Swindon Town – *Salubritas et industria* Healthiness and industry

Tottenham Hotspur – *Audere est facere* To dare is to do

Tranmere Rovers – *Ubi fides ibi lux et robur* Where there is faith there is light and strength

Watford – *Audentior* More daring

The mediterranean lands have always been blessed with much better weather than those of northern Europe. As a result they tend to have a culture which is more 'al fresco' than our own. If you're spending a lot of time out of doors you need a general meeting place. In Greece this was the *Agora* and in Roman towns the *Forum*. This is often translated as 'the market place' but this is to misunderstand the way of life in these cultures. The **Forum** certainly was the place where markets would take place, but it was much more than that. It was the central location where public things happened. It was the market, the pub, the village hall, the church, the local newspaper and the law courts all rolled into one.

As a result it is not surprising that we can find a lot of echoes of the Forum in English, not least of which being our use of the word Forum itself as a general talking shop or chat room.

The Latin adjective *forensis*, relating to the Forum, gives us **forensic**, a word we use to refer to things connected to the law and the proving of crimes as in **forensic pathologist**. The link comes from the fact that the law courts were situated on one side of the Forum.

You may feel uncomfortable in such a large open space like this. If you do, you suffer from **agoraphobia**, a fear of open spaces. This comes from the Greek *agora*. (The spelling 'agora' shows that the word has nothing to do with the Latin word for field '*agro*' a common misconception.)

The Romans were pretty hot in the area of public toilets and were much less inhibited than we are. They were also very practical and did recycling in a way that we would not contemplate today. Put the two activities together and, you guessed it... the average Forum would have at least one large vessel in a corner somewhere as a piss pot, placed there by the local fulling business to collect urine since it is an excellent substance for treating raw wool before making it into **textiles** (Lat. *textilis* = woven). This word also gives us **text** and **texture**. The kind of sponsorship deals from clothes manufacturers on the piss pots can only be imagined.

A Roman town would have periodic markets in the same way that we do today. They would have been a mixture of food and household goods with local and travelling traders bringing their **produce** to sell (Lat. *produco* = I bring out) and peasant farmers bringing in seasonal food. The word **market** itself derives from the Latin word *mercatus* meaning bought, which also gives us the word **merchant**. Of course, traders both buy and sell and in the sales role they are **vendors** (Lat. *vendere* = sell).

In Rome, in particular, some of the traders would be foreigners with **imports** (Lat. *importare* = carry in) from the **provinces** (Lat. *provinciae* = put in chains).

To give you a hand in the buying process the Greeks and the Romans developed sophisticated systems of weights and measures. The Roman system was based on the pound, which was divided into twelve parts or *unciae*, our **ounce**. The Latin for pound was *libra* but the word **pound** ultimately derives from the Latin *pondus* weight.

Early currency systems used small amounts of precious metals which were weighed to determine their value. The legacy of this method remains in the word **spend** from the Latin *expendere*, to weigh.

All traders were supervised by local officials called *aediles* whose principal purpose was to levy **taxes** (Lat. *taxare* = to charge).

Around the Forum's **perimeter** (Gk. *peri* = around + *metron* = measure) there would have been the everyday shops that surround our own market places. They would be selling anything from pots and pans to bread, clothes and slaves. There would also have been plenty of **taverns** (Lat. *tabernae)*, either for eating in or taking away. If you think that McDonalds is a new phenomenon, think again. Fast food was just as popular with the Romans as it is with us. At Herculaneum there is a very well-preserved shop containing a long stone counter with holes in the top. This would probably have been something akin to a modern cafe with big bowls of food sitting in the holes and tables and chairs all around.

The Forum was a **public** place (Lat. *publicus* = belonging to the people), so it was the ideal place to **publicise** (Lat. *publicare*) news from home and abroad. Such **reports** (Lat. *reportare* = bring back) might be nailed up on boards or announced by a town crier, an early version of a newsreader.

Getting one's money's worth

On market days you would be wise to look carefully at anything before you bought it. *Caveat emptor* was a principle of any Roman market and it is also engrained in our own legal system. It means simply 'let the buyer beware'. The seller puts his goods on offer after which point it is up to the buyer to decide if they are: a) what the seller says they are and b) if the asking price is acceptable. This is still the principle that governs shopping today whether we are in Marks & Spencer or dealing with a second-hand car salesman.

Gardening or **horticulture** (Lat. *hortus* = garden + *cultura* = cultivation) was introduced to Britain by the Romans and ever since, botanists have used Latin to classify plants according to their **genus** (Lat. = birth) and **species** (Lat. = appearance). This may be a very good academic system but it has little relevance to today's ordinary gardener. On the other hand, many of the common and much-loved flowers that adorn our gardens have generic Greek and Latin names that we are happy to use quite freely.

Here is a selection.

Amaryllis (Gk. *amarullis* = a girl's name). Originally from Southern Africa, this is a late-flowering lily. The name Amarullis was a general one in Greek and Roman poetry for a rustic maiden.

Anemone (Gk. *anemóné* from *anemos* = wind). The wind flower, so called because its hardiness enables it to survive in tough environments.

Aster (Gk. *astér* = star). The Michaelmas daisy. The petal formation of the daisies resembles the classic pattern we use to depict twinkling stars.

Chrysanthemum (Gk. *khrusos* = gold + *anthemon* = flower). Although hybrid species come in all shapes and colours, the yellow varieties must have been the favourites for the Greeks.

Convolvulus (Lat. *con* = with + *volvere* = roll). A menace to all gardeners, this plant rolls itself around the stems of others and if unchecked can choke the plants it grows on.

Crocus (Gk. *krokos* = the purple crocus). The Greek word refered specifically to the purple flower. In ancient times purple was an expensive dye to obtain so it was a much prized colour used in clothing to mark out high status.

Delphinium (Gk. *delphinion* = larkspur, diminutive of *delphis* = dolphin). Larkspur is one of the family of Delphiniums, its flowers resembling the shape of a dolphin. In my mind delphiniums are inextricably linked with geraniums. If you have never read *The Dormouse and the Doctor* by AA Milne, you have missed out on one of the most charming of children's poems. It vindicates the small man's (or, in this case, dormouse's) struggle and final victory against authority with its backdrop of 'Delphiniums blue and geraniums red'.

Digitalis (Lat. *digitus* = finger). A flower that has a number of popular names although foxglove is much the most common. Perhaps the strangest too; why on earth should we consider letting foxes have gloves? 'Thimble-flower' seems much more appropriate.

Garden flowers

Geranium (Gk. *geranos* = crane). Lovely flowers but I've never seen their resemblance to a crane. I suppose the stems do grow quite long, though.

Gladiolus (Lat. diminutive of *gladius* = sword). Dame Edna's favourite flower is so called because its leaves resemble the shape of a sword.

Hebe (A greek goddess). Hebe, a daughter of Zeus and Hera, was the personification of eternal youth. Even after years in poor soil conditions hebes can still look splendid.

Helianthus (Gk. *helios* = sun + *anthos* = flower). The common sunflower. In the major growing areas of Italy and France the flowers are called *tornasole* and *tournesoleil* respectively because of their tendency to turn towards the sun. In fact, most flowers turn towards the sun and this characteristic was singled out by the Greeks for the **heliotrope** (Gk. *helios* = sun + *tropos* = turned), a shrub with fragrant purple flowers.

Hyacinth (Gk. *huakinthos* = a species of blue larkspur). A flower that supposedly sprang from the blood of Hyacinthus, a youth loved by Apollo who accidentally killed him with an unlucky throw of a discus. Seriously unlucky!

Impatiens (Lat. = impatient). Commonly called the busy lizzie, which seems to be a misunderstanding of the meaning of *impatiens*. The flower is also called 'touch-me-not' which is the real sense of the Latin name since its seed pods, when ripe, will burst open at the slightest touch – the seeds are impatient to get out.

Iris (Gk. *Iris* = the goddess of the rainbow). The striking yellow and blue colours of the flowers present a vibrant reminder of rainbow colours.

Lily (Lat. *lilium* from Gk. *leirion*). A much loved genus of species related on one hand to rushes and on the other to the amaryllis.

Narcissus (Gk. *Narkissos*). Narkissos was a youth who pined away for the love of his own reflection in the water and was transformed into a daffodil. A link has been made with the Greek word *narké* meaning numbness because the flower has 'narcotic' effects, but this is probably fanciful. I've never eaten one myself.

Phlox (Gk. = flame). Wallflowers come in a variety of colours but to the Greeks the finest were the bright reds and oranges.

Polyanthus (Gk. *poly* = many + *anthos* = flower). The cultivated primrose, which is also called **primula** (Lat. diminutive of *primus* first) because it is one of the first flowers of spring to appear.

Mesmebryanthemum
(Gk. *mesémbria* = noon + *anthemon* = flower).

Plants from southern Africa whose flowers have the good sense to wait until noon before opening. I once found myself in a small flower shop in the middle of Italy looking for a pot plant. I settled for a Mesembryanthemum and asked the florist what its name was in Italian. 'Mi sembra un treno' was the reply. On seeing my look of astonishment he added, 'I know it's strange but that's what we call it round these parts.' Strange? It's barking mad to call a flower 'I think I'm a train'. A case of Chinese Whispers do you suppose? Or was he just having a laugh?

If you fancy doing some empire building then it helps to have a fairly good idea of where you are going. The Greek empire, built up by Alexander the Great, covered the largest geographical area that had ever existed under the control of one domain. It was too vast to control and quickly fell apart. The Roman empire that followed lasted for much longer. In both cases, understanding the **geography** of the lands they were trying to conquer was vital (Gk. *gé* = earth + *graphó* = writing).

Acropolis (Gk. *akron* = summit + *polis* = city). The upper part of a fortified city. We know the acropolis as the imposing hill in the centre of Athens where the Parthenon stands. In fact, many other Greek cities had a similar high place called the acropolis, which was a citadel or hill fort that was easily defended.

Amazon (Gk. *a* = no + *mazon* = breast). This word was originally ascribed to certain tribes in Scythia (modern Kazakhstan) who had warrior women. It was reputed that the female warriors would have their right breast removed to facilitate the use of a bow in warfare. Ancient depictions show women with the right breast covered to protect it and this seems the likely derivation. The world's longest river was so named by a spanish soldier, Francisco de Orellana, in the 1540s after he had seen female warriors with bows there.

Arctic (Gk. *arktikos* = of a bear). The Greek derivation owes nothing to an intrepid ancient traveller on a trip to the North Pole who stumbled on polar bears. It relates to the principal northern constellation Ursa Major, which the Greeks also called the Great Bear and which points to Ursa Minor and the Pole Star. Keep following the bears and you eventually get to the Arctic.

Atlas. In Greek mythology the Titans were a race of giants from whom the humans were descended. One of them, Atlas, was said to bear the heavens on his shoulders. The modern meaning derives from an early book of maps which had as its title plate a drawing of Atlas, in his familiar pose, only now with the earth on his shoulders. The word **Atlantic** is also derived from Atlas, as is the mountain range of northwest Africa. These were thought to be the natural manifestation of Atlas so the ocean beyond was called by the same name.

Bosporus (Gk. *bous* = cow + *poros* = ford). The Bosporus is the strait in western Turkey that separates Asia from Europe. It connects the Black Sea with the Sea of Marmara. The name comes from one of the many amorous adventures of the god Zeus who in this case had his eye on a girl called Io. In order to deceive his wife, Hera, Zeus changed Io into a white cow that swam across the Bosporos to escape.

Cincinnati (Lat. *Cincinnatus* = a legendary hero). Cincinnatus embodies the American dream. A Roman who rose from being a simple farmer to become Consul, delivered his country from a bunch of thugs, retired and went back to ploughing. The city in Ohio which bears his name was so called by the President of the Cincinnati, a society of officers created after the peace of 1783 to assist the injured in the US war of Independence.

Delta. The word is used to describe an area where a large river splits up into many streams and mudflats as it enters the sea, thanks to its resemblance to the capital version of the Greek letter delta, $\triangle$.

Equator (Lat. *aequatus* = made equal). The ancients understood that the sun is directly overhead at the equator on the equinoxes, and thus surmised that this point must be the mid-way between the two halves of the earth.

Europe. Another of Zeus's indiscretions which must have been a pretty big one to have a whole continent named after it. The girl in question this time was Europa. Zeus

Leabharlanna Fhine Gall

turned himself into a bull and carried her on his back all the way to Crete. Which I suppose makes Crete the capital of Europe.

Germany (Lat. *germania*). A name given by the Romans to a large area of central and northern Europe. In fact, to a Roman, you go north over the Alps and wherever you end up, provided you're not in Gaul (France), you're in Germany. The word may have a Celtic origin meaning nothing more precise than neighbour.

Hellespont (Gk *hellés* = Greek + *pontos* = sea). Beyond the Bosporus is the Dardanelles, formerly called the Hellespont, which connects the Sea of Marmara to the Aegean sea. In an attempt to emulate the legendary character Leander who swam across it to visit his sweetheart, the priestess Hero, Lord Byron swam the straits in 1810 when aged 22.

Isthmus (Gk. *isthmos* = neck). A narrow piece of land which connects two neighbouring pieces of land.

Langue d'oc and **Langue d'oil**. In France, the Langue d'oc is the area to the south of the Loire, whereas the Langue d'oil is the area to the north. The difference comes from a time when the two regions spoke different dialects and had different words for 'yes'. The d'oc used the Latin *hoc* (this) the d'oil used the Latin *illud* (that) as in 'this is it' or 'that's right'.

Mediterranean (Lat. *medius* = middle + *terra* = land). The Greeks and Romans were excellent navigators and were passable map makers so they knew that the sea beyond their shores lay between the Northern, European part, and the Southern, African part of the known world. Knowing the Latin derivation helps you to remember the right number of ts, rs and ns, when spelling the word.

Mesopotamia (Gk. *meso* = middle + *potamos* = river). This ancient kingdom equates roughly to modern Iraq and covers the area between the two great Middle Eastern rivers, the Tigris and the Euphrates.

Philadelphia (Gk. *philo* = love + *adelphos* = brother). The first city of the state of Pennsylvania was founded by William Penn and the society of friends who considered brotherly love an appropriate title.

Pillars of Hercules. The two rocks at either side of the Atlantic entrance to the Mediterranean sea, which today we name as Gibraltar and Mount Hacho in Morocco. Legend tells that they were bound together until Hercules ripped them apart.

Pangaea (Gk. *pan* = all + *gaia* = earth). These days we are well aware of plate tectonics and the way that the landmasses ride on subterranean plates. Scientists have postulated a period in time when the alignment of the plates was such that before they started to move apart all the land masses were contained in one super continent called Pangaea. Alternatively, it is the name of the night club in Piccadilly where Prince Harry famously came to blows with paparazzi in the summer of 2004.

Peninsula (Lat. *paene* = almost + *insula* = island). A strip of land that juts out into the water and is almost an island. It can be huge, such as the **Iberian** peninsula comprising the whole of Spain and Portugal (Lat. *Hiberia* = Spain). The Peninsular War (1808-1814) refers to the hostilities between Britain and Napoleon on the Iberian peninsula.

Terra firma (Lat. = solid land). Rather than solid land we tend to use the expression dry land. This is slightly ironic given how damp our climate tends to be.

Rival (Lat. *rivalis* = of a riverman)

It is not immediately obvious that this word has a geographical context but it originally referred to people living on the opposite sides of a river. In ancient, and not so ancient, times the right to a stretch of river was keenly fought over. Not only do rivers form natural boundaries, they are very fruitful and control of them gives rise to much rivalry.

The Gaia Theory

Gaia was a Greek goddess who was the embodiment of all things concerned with the earth. Her name is the basis of all the ge- words like geography, geology and geometry. Her name was also used as the title of a theory devised in the 1960s by James Lovelock who was doing work for NASA on methods for detecting life on Mars.

His hypothesis runs like this: life as a whole on earth maintains an environment that is suitable for its continued existence, and the nature of all the interrelated systems of the Earth creates a benevolent existence for the creatures that live on it.

Since he first proposed the idea it has been hotly debated by scientists in many fields. Not least because it predicts that global warming can't happen.

A different model suggests that planet earth can look after itself but that the individual species that come and go are pretty transitory. So when a massive asteroid smashed into the Gulf of Mexico 65 million years ago, creating a crater approximately 180 kilometres in diameter, there followed something akin to a long nuclear winter that wiped out thousands of species including most of the dinosaurs.

After a brief period of time planet Earth simply got up, dusted itself down and just got on with things pretty much as usual (only without the dinosaurs).

And so it may be with mankind. We may be capable of self-destruction either through nuclear warfare or being unable to survive the climate change that we have probably inflicted on ourselves, or we may be wiped out by the same sort of equally apocalyptic event that did for the dinosaurs. Planet Earth will simply say goodnight to the human species (without too many tears) and will just keep on going until another dominant species takes over and is killed off in its turn.

Ocean (Gk. *ókeanus* = a figure in mythology)

Ókeanus was a child of Ouranus and Gaia (who themselves represented heaven and earth). He was the oldest of the Titans, a race of giants that were the first people on earth (Atlas was one of his younger brothers). He was the personification of the sea and the children he had with Tethys were the race of sea-nymphs.

Geography

The Pacific Ocean

(Lat. *pacis* = peace + *facere* = make)

Many of the names we use today for places around the globe date back to the age of the great European explorers and adventurers. The Pacific ocean was named by the Portuguese explorer Ferdinand Magellan, working for the Spanish king Philip II. He was trying to find the southwest passage that might link the northern and the southern seas (what we know today as the Atlantic and the Pacific). The name Pacific did not arise from the friendliness of the people he encountered (just look at the fearsome nature of the hakka performed by the Pacific nations before rugby internationals). It came from something that was more like a eureka moment. Magellan did eventually find a passage from the Atlantic to the Pacific through the southern tip of Chile, a passage which is still called after him, the Straits of Magellan. His passage through the straits was so tempestuous that when Magellan's fleet finally broke free from the coast of Chile and they entered the calmer waters of the open ocean, the captain, in his relief, named the sea 'pacific'. Unfortunately, the area was anything but peaceful and not long afterwards Magellan was killed in the

Philippines (which, incidentally, were named after his boss, Philip of Spain).

The name Pacific did not immediately take off and the great expanse of water was still referred to as the South Sea. By the 18th century, Pacific had become the popular term, as can be seen in the 1776 account by John Ledyard entitled 'A journal of Captain Cook's Last Voyage to the Pacific Ocean'.

The various groupings of islands in the Pacific are all derived from the Greek word for island, *nésos*. **Indonesia** are the Indian islands, **Polynesia** means many islands, **Micronesia** is a group of islands, all of which are small, and **Melanesia**, black islands, refers to the dark skin colour of the natives.

The biggest island of them all, **Australia**, comes from the Latin *australis* from *Auster*, the personification of the south wind.

Geology (Gk. *gé* = earth + *logos* = understanding) is the study of the rocks which make up the earth's **crust** (Lat. *crusta* = rind). Over time **sedimentary** rocks (Lat. *sedimentum* = settlement) are laid down at the bottom of seas and oceans and **igneous** rocks (Lat. *ignis* = fire) are formed by lava flows (Volcanoes q.v.). By studying the **fossil** record (Lat. *fossum* = dug up) in the various **strata** (Lat. *stratum* = laid down) geologists chart the record of the earth's **evolution** (Lat. *evolutio* = unrolling). I have included those ages which do not have Greek or Latin roots because it would be a rather strange table otherwise.

The Periods of the Palaeozoic Era

(Gk. *palaios* + *zóé* = old life)

Cambrian *600m* (Lat. *Cambria* = Wales).

Ordovician *500m* (Ordovices – Roman name for a tribe of north Wales).

Silurian *440m* (Silures – Roman name for a tribe on the Welsh border).

Devonian *400m* (Simply named after Devon) First land plants appear.

Carboniferous *350m* (Lat. *carbonis* + *ferre* = carry coal). Amphibians, insects and coal.

Geological ages

Permian *270m* (Named after Perm in Russia). First mammals.

The Periods of the **Mesozoic** Era

(Gk. *meso + zóé* = middle life)

Triassic *225m* (Gk. *trias* = a group of three, signifying the three distinct rock layers found.)
Jurassic *180m* (Named after the Jura mountains between France and Switzerland.)
Cretaceous *135m* (Lat. *cretaceus* = chalky). Ends in the extinction of the dinosaurs.

The Periods of the **Cainozoic** Era

(Gk. *kainos + zóé* = recent life)

This era covers the time from the extinction of the dinosaurs to the modern day. It is made up of two periods, the Paleogene and the Neogene, each divided into three epochs.

Palaeogene *65m – 23m*
(Gk. *palaios + genea* = ancient birth).
The relevance of 'birth' refers to the fact that the period as a whole is about the development of modern flora and fauna.

Palaeocene *65m – 55m* (Gk. *palaios* + *kainos* = ancient recent). The oldest epoch in this period. New fauna fill niches left by the extinction of the dinosaurs.

Eocene *55m – 34m* (Gk. *eos* + *kainos* = dawn of recent). The first mammals appear in large numbers.

Oligocene *34m – 23m* (Gk. *oligos* + *kainos* = few recent). Scarcity of new species after the bursting forth of new species in the Eocene.

Neogene *23m – 0.01m* (Gk. *neos* + *genea* = new birth). The second period of this era is notable for significant evolution among mammals and birds.

Miocene *23m – 5m* (Gk. *meion* + *kainos* = less recent). This epoch contains fewer modern sea invertebrates than appear in the Pleisotcene.

Pliocene *5m – 2m* (Gk. *pleion* + *kainos* = more recent). Named because the marine mollusc faunas are fairly similar to today.

Pleistocene *2m – 0.01m* (Gk. *pleistos* + *kainos* = most recent). The age of early man.

The epoch in which we now live has for a long time been

referred to as the **Holocene** which began around 10,000 BC. It is named after the Greek word *holos*, meaning whole or entire, so the name translates as 'entirely recent'. However, in the wake of global warming and climate change some scientists have suggested that the holocene ended around AD1800 with the beginning of the Industrial Revolution and the move towards our increased use of fossil fuels. They propose calling the new epoch in which we live today the **anthropocene** (Gk. *anthrópos* + *kainos* = mankind recent).

The numbers indicate the number of years ago, in millions, that each period began, and, for the Cainozoic era, show total duration.

The word **Geometry** is derived from two Greek words, *gé* earth and *metron* measure. It may seem a bit of a leap from classroom geometry with its triangles, angles and cosines to measuring the earth but stick with it for a moment.

Greek astronomers knew that the earth was round from observing the shadow it casts on the moon during a lunar eclipse, but they didn't know how big it was until around 200 BC when Eratosthenes discovered a way to measure the earth's circumference. He had heard reports that in the city of Syene (modern-day Aswan in Egypt), the sun shone directly down vertical wells on the summer solstice. This never happened in Alexandria, Eratosthenes' home town, since Syene was on the Tropic of Cancer whereas Alexandria was some way to the north. So on the first day of summer, Eratosthenes measured the angle of the sun in Alexandria and found that it was 7° from the vertical. Based on this observation he reasoned that the distance between Syene and Alexandria must be 7/360 of the earth's circumference. (The idea that a circle is made up of 360 degrees was already commonplace.) He then worked out the distance between Alexandria and Syene as around 5000 stades. (A stade was a Greek measurement from which we also get the word Stadium see Playgrounds). When he multiplied the distance from Alexandria to Syene by 360/7 the answer came to just over 250,000 stades or around 42,000 km. The modern value for the circumference of the earth is 40,000 km, so Eratosthenes' calculation was within 5% of what we know today.

One innovation the Greeks brought to mathematics and **geometry** was the concept of proof. And nowhere is this better exemplified than in Pythagoras' theorem. Pythagoras, as a historical person, is barely recorded but his theorem has been spouted by generations of schoolchildren the world over:

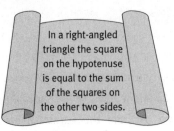

In a right-angled triangle the square on the hypotenuse is equal to the sum of the squares on the other two sides.

Hypotenuse comes from two Greek words meaning to stretch underneath. In a right-angled triangle it is the longest side. If the triangle is depicted thus:

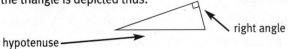

right angle

hypotenuse

the idea of stretching underneath becomes clear. The idea that underlies Pythagoras' Theorem almost certainly predated Greek civilisation, but it is probable that it was the Greeks who first worked out how to prove it.

Proving Pythagoras' Theorem...the easy way

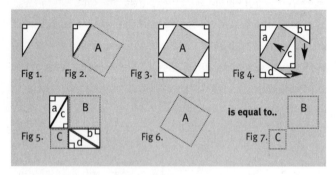

1. Take a right-angled triangle (Fig 1.)
2. Draw a square on the hypotenuse, square A (Fig. 2)
3. Draw another three identical triangles around square A (Fig 3)
4. Rearrange the triangles by moving c to a, b down and d across (Fig 4.)
5. The rearrangement in Fig. 5 covers the same area as Fig. 3. This has created two new squares: B the square on the longer side of the triangle and C the square on the shorter side.
6. Remove the triangles from both Fig. 3 and Fig. 5 to leave Fig. 6 and Fig. 7
7. The areas bounded by Fig 3. and Fig 5. cover an identical area. So when the triangles are removed what is left must also cover an identical area.

Hence: **The square on the hypotenuse (Fig. 6) is equal to the sum of the squares on the other two sides (Fig. 7).**

...got it...

Another famed Greek mathematician was Archimedes. He reasoned that if he got into a bathtub which was full to the brim, then the amount of water that ended up on the bathroom floor would be the same as his own body mass. (Probably best not to try this at home.) Whether his exclamation of '*Eureka*' (Gk. = I have found it) related to his sudden realisation of the concept or his delight in finally finding the bathroom is not recorded.

Girls' Names

Agatha (Gr.) virtuous

Agnes (Gr.) pure

Amanda (Lat.) to be loved

Angelina (Gr.) messenger

Arabella (Lat.) beautiful altar

Aurelia (Lat.) golden

Aurora (Lat.) dawn

Barbara (Lat.) foreign

Bernice (Gr.) bringing victory

Camilla (Lat.) attendant at sacrifice

Candida (Lat.) white

Catherine (Gr.) peaceful

Cecilia, Celia (Lat.) poor-sighted

Charity (Lat.) grace

Chloe (Gr.) young plant

Christina (Gr.) follower of Christ

Clara (Lat.) bright

Diana (Gr.) goddess of hunting

Doris (Gr.) gift

Dorothy (Gr.) gift of god

Emilia (Lat.) rival

Eugenia (Gr.) well-born

Felicity (Lat.) lucky

Gemma (Lat.) jewel

Georgia (Gk.) farmer

Grace (Lat.) goodwill

Irene (Gr.) peace

Julia (Lat.) soft-haired

Laura (Lat.) laurel

Lavinia (Lat.) of Latin race

Letitia (Lat.) joy

Lilian (Lat.) lily

Lucy (Lat.) shining

Margaret (Gr.) pearly

Olivia (Lat.) olive tree

Ophelia (Gr.) help

Penelope (Gr.) weaver

Philippa (Gr.) lover of horses

Phoebe (Gr.) light of life

Phyllis (Gr.) foliage

Girls' Names

Priscilla (Lat.) ancient

Rhoda (Gr.) rose coloured

Rita (Gk.) pearl

Selina (Gr.) full moon

Sibylla (Gr.) prophetess

Sophia (Gr.) wisdom

Sylvia (Lat.) woodland

Thea (Gr.) goddess

Ursula (Lat.) little bear

Veronica (Gk.) victory bringer

Victoria (Lat.) victory

Zoe (Gr.) life

Norma. This name has one of the strangest of all derivations. It is not the female equivalent of Norman (man from the North), but means the expected standard or what is correct. *Norma* is the Latin word for a carpenter's square used for measuring right angles. (It also, of course, gives us the words **norm** and **normal**.)

Comedy (Gk. *komos* + *ódé* = revelling song)

Early Greek comedy consisted of bawdy songs associated with fertility festivals and village revels.

The Greek philosopher Aristotle believed that comedy originated in phallic songs and later gained the more refined objectives of satire and generally poking fun at people.

Certainly innuendo and a bit of smut is in the true spirit of the genre.

Tragedy (Gk. *tragos* + *ódé* = goat song)

Although the derivation of this word is clear it is not understood why tragedy and goats should be linked in the Greek mind. The end for many a goat was to have its throat cut as a sacrificial victim, so that's pretty tragic for the goat.

It may well have been down to the fact that victorious actors in tragic drama contests received a goat as a prize.

Melodrama (Gk. *melos* + *drama* = a play with song). Melodramas follow a basic formula of a villain posing a threat, the hero escaping or rescuing the heroine, all followed by a happy ending. Music is used to heighten the emotional intensity. Many silent films were

melodramas, accompanied by a pianist in the cinema.
Put the two Greek words for song, *melos* and *ódé*,
together and you have melody.

Parody (Gk. *para* + *ódé* = song beyond)

A parody was literally a song that perverted the true
meaning of another song. We use it today to refer to any
kind of writing or drama that is an exaggerated copy of the
thing it is poking fun at – something that goes beyond its
true nature.

The Greek Alphabet

For ease of reading, the Greek words in this book have been transliterated into the Roman alphabet. From time to time, however, the Greek letters themselves have a relevance so this page is devoted to them. (The word **alphabet** is formed from the first two Greek letters *alpha* and *beta*.)

It is interesting to note that, as in the Roman alphabet, upper and lower case letters in the Greek alphabet are notably different in appearance. This stems largely from the fact that inscriptions in stone are easier to carve with simple broad strokes. Lower case letters were developed when handwriting became the norm on wax tablets or papyrus. The Greek word *papuros*, a kind of bullrush, is the root for our word **paper**.

Here are some instances of the names of Greek letters in use:

'I am the beginning and the end' said the Lord. 'The *Alpha* and the *Omega*'.

Among many species, the leading male in a tribe is referred to as the *Alpha* male. The International Phonetic alphabet includes two letters, *Alpha* and *Delta*, we use *iota* to mean a very small amount and Fraternity Houses in

The Greek Alphabet

Ivy League Universities use combinations of three Greek letters as names.
Greek letters are also extensively used in mathematics and physics.

In Aldous Huxley's novel, *Brave New World*, the people are ranked in a caste system using the first five letters, *Alpha*, *Beta*, *Gamma*, *Delta* and *Epsilon*. Huxley took the title of the book from a phrase in Shakespeare's play, *The Tempest*. Prospero's daughter, Miranda, has led a very sheltered life, so when she suddenly encounters a group of new people, she excitedly pronounces: 'Oh brave new world that has such people in it'. During the play Ferdinand, upon learning her name, exclaims 'Admired Miranda', a verbal pun in which Shakespeare makes use of the fact that the name is in its original Latin form. Miranda is a gerundive (a verbal adjective) and means a female that is to be looked at in wonder or 'admired'.

The Greek Alphabet

The Alphabet

A	α	alpha	I	ι	iota	P	ρ	rho
B	β	beta	K	κ	kappa	Σ	σ	sigma
Γ	γ	gamma	Λ	λ	lambda	T	τ	tau
Δ	δ	delta	M	μ	mu	Υ	υ	upsilon
E	ε	epsilon	N	ν	nu	Φ	φ	phi
Z	ζ	zeta	Ξ	ξ	xi	X	χ	khi
H	η	eta	O	o	omicron	Ψ	ψ	psi
Θ	ϑ	theta	Π	π	pi	Ω	ω	omega

There are various medical practitioners who deal with aspects of healing that tend to use hands-on procedures rather than resorting to medicines.

Acupuncturist (Lat. *acu* = with a needle + *punctura* = piercing). Originally a Chinese medical technique, the Romans practiced **auricular** acupuncture (Lat. = of the ear), placing needles in various points in the ear.

Chiropractor (Gk. *kheiros* = hand + *praktikos* = acting on). Someone who manipulates bones, especially those of the spinal column, to cure certain ills.

Chiropodist (Gk. *kheiropodés* = with chapped feet). Curiously, the origin of this word is totally different from that of chiropractor. It is not *kheiros* meaning hand but *kheirón* meaning worse and *podos*, foot, found together in a compound word meaning having bad feet.

Podiatrist (Gk. *podos* = foot + *iatros* = physician). This, in essence, is exactly the same as a chiropodist. It is an American term.

Dietician (Gk. *diaita* = a way of living). A strict diet can indeed become a way of life.

Homoeopath (Gk. *omoios* = like + *pathos* = suffering). Someone who treats a patient with tiny amounts of a drug that in a healthy individual would produce the symptoms the patient is suffering.

Hypnotherapist (Gk. *hupnos* = sleep + *therapeia* = therapy). Hypnotism usually does not actually send the patient to sleep but induces a deep calm at which point they are highly suggestible.

Orthodontist (Gk. *orthos* = straight + Lat. *dentis* = tooth). A portmanteau word formed from one Latin word and one Greek word, a clear indication that the word is a modern invention rather than an occupation that the Romans or Greeks would have known.

Osteopath (Gk. *osteon* = bone + *pathos* = suffering). One who treats ailments through focusing on the body's skeleton and joint function.

Veterinary surgeon (Lat. *veterinarius* = of cattle). So perhaps without realising it, the fact that the TV programme *All Creatures Great and Small* always seemed to revolve around the posteriors of cattle is totally apt to the essence of being a vet.

What is the difference between?

Psychiatrist (Gk. *psukhé* = soul + *iatros* = physician) and
Psychologist (Gk. *psukhé* = soul + *logos* = knowledge)?

The difference between these two practitioners is that the
first aims to heal your inner self, the second only aims to
understand it.

A **psychoanalyst** (Gk. *analusis* = freeing up) is an
American term for someone who frees up the contents
of a patient's wallet.

'History,' as Henry Ford famously put it, 'is more or less bunk'. Nonetheless, plenty of people have chosen to record events and suggest the motives that people have had for their actions. So some folks must find it pretty interesting, Henry.

Asterix. Although the comic book character Asterix the Gaul is a purely fictional creation, he does have a basis in reality. While Julius Caesar was conquering Gaul (modern France) a rebellion broke out in 52BC led by a chieftain of the Arverni tribe called Vercingetorix. This was effectively the last resistance that Caesar encountered. The -ix ending was common in that part of Gaul and was used in the Asterix books to make amusing names like the magic-potion making Druid, Getafix.

Aeon (Gk. *aion* = age). There always seems to be a deal of confusion about how this word is spelt, particularly among crossword compilers. Is it aeon or eon? Its Greek origin would suggest the former. It means the largest division of geological time.

Anachronism (Gk. *ana* = backwards + *khronos* = time). Something that does not belong to that part of time in which it is found e.g. an actor's wristwatch in a Jane Austen period drama.

Antediluvian (Lat. *ante* = before + *diluvium* = deluge). Incredibly old. It is unclear how the story of the Flood came about but as it appears in many different cultures it must have been a pretty catastrophic period which involved a rise in the sea level. The word refers to the fact that the flood appears early in the Bible so anything before it is very ancient indeed.

Epoch (Gk. *epokhé* = stoppage). The word epoch has a specific meaning that has been gradually eroded through usage. It originally meant the point at which an era in history came to an end and a new one began, or a period in history marked by special events.

Herodotus. The so-called Father of History. I studied part of Herodotus' history as part of my A-level syllabus and I have to say I rather enjoyed it (partly because it was the only class we shared with the girls' school next door). Writing in the fifth century BC, his book looks at the origins of the Persian invasions into Greece between 490 and 480 BC.

Magna Carta (Lat. = great paper). The Latin *carta* comes from the Greek word *khartés,* meaning papyrus leaf. This **Charter,** published in 1215, sought to define property rights across England under King John and is one of the most important documents in the history of democracy.

Plantagenet (Lat. *planta* = plant + *genesta* = broom). The name of the English kings from Henry II to Richard III. It is generally thought that the nickname goes back to Henry II's father, Geoffrey of Anjou, who supposedly wore a sprig of broom in his hat. Another possible reason was that he planted broom to provide a cover crop to improve his hunting estates.

Our holidays are one of the highlights of the year. Sun, sand, salmonella... whatever. It's something to look forward to, a well-earned break, time off for good behaviour. The one thing we shy away from is calling it a **vacation**. Why ever not? the Latin word *vaccatio* (= freedom) is where the French get 'vacances' and the Italians 'vacanza'. Simply put, it means freedom. Freedom from having to turn up every day for work, perhaps. By the time of Tacitus, a Roman historian who was writing during a particularly corrupt period of the Empire, the word *vaccatio* had taken on a more sinister meaning of a payment to exempt a person from military duty. A bribe in fact. So is this the reason we shun the word vacation and use holiday instead, with its connotations of being a holy day? Nope. It's the pure snobbery associated with the fact that we don't like to use words that we associate with our American cousins, who we still think should be taking words from us and not vice versa.

But enough of that. If we are leaving these shores for a holivac abroad we will start from some kind of **port** (Lat. *portus* = a harbour). Whether you are flying, sailing or taking the Chunnel, you will be taking your **passport** (Lat. *passus* = a step), which literally lets you step out on your grand journey. These days your passport may include

biometric information (Gk. *bios* = life + *metron* = measurement) and you may need a **visa** (Lat. = seen) to confirm to the people you are visiting that you are **bona fide** (Lat. = in good faith). That may or may not hold good for your plastic. So take Amex or Mastercard as well to be on the safe side. If you are driving you may well need a **map**, from the Latin *mappa* meaning a napkin, a rather appropriate derivation since the map spends most if its time covering your lap. The best known occurence of the Latin word is the *Mappa Mundi*, a 13th-century map of the world painted on vellum parchment now in Hereford cathedral. Once you have arrived at your **destination** (Lat. *destinatio* = appointment), you will probably need a **transfer** (Lat. *transferre* = carry across) to wherever you are staying before you finally get a chance to **relax** (Lat. *relaxare* = loosen up).

Provided you have not lost it on your journey, there is every chance that you will have a **camera** with you. With a digital camera these days it is just point, shoot, brilliant **photograph** (Gk. *phótos* = light + *graphó* = write). But you are well advised to take a step back if you are holidaying in Italy. If you start talking to an Italian waiter about your camera you'll either get a dodgy look or find yourself being propositioned, depending on whether you are male or female – since camera is the Italian for room and to an Italian waiter, bedroom in particular.

So what is the link between the two, or rather, when the photographic camera was invented why did it take its name from an Italian/Latin word which means room?

Well, bedroom antics apart, we need to take a step back to the age of the Victorians and the circus trick that was known as the **Camera Obscura** (Lat. = dark vaulted room). Set up at the top of high buildings surrounding public parks or at fair grounds, the Camera Obscura was a domed room housing a lens system that could be trained on the public parading in the area below and project the image onto a table in the middle of the room. This enabled the viewers inside to watch the antics that were going on below without being seen themselves. The British flocked to this amusement in their droves hoping for a saucy glimpse of a courting couple in the bushes who would be blissfully unaware that they had been caught on the first version of candid camera and the name for a way of capturing images stuck. For the Italians it still means the room, not the apparatus (which, incidentally, is called a 'macchina photographica' or light writing machine.)

Two of Europe's favourite capitals

The origin of... Paris

Paris was the son of Priam, King of Troy, and, as the instigator of the Trojan War, has a lot to answer for. One of the things for which he cannot be called to account is the name of the capital of France. This comes from the name of the original Celtic tribe – the Parisii. To the Romans, Paris was known as *Lutetia Parisiorum*, meaning the mudtown of the Parisii.

The origin of... Rome

You may feel that this one is distinctly out of left field, but Rome was not named after Romulus. The story of Romulus and Remus, the two orphans suckled by a she-wolf who then went on to found Rome, is a cute story and well known to the Romans as well as us. It's just not true. The city was named after the Greek word *rómé*, which means strength. Confirmation comes from a lesser known title of Rome, *Valentia*, from the Latin word *valens* meaning strong.

Home and family

Domesticity, how we love it. The word **domestic** (Lat. *domus* = house) refers to anything concerned with the home environment. I can never look at the word *domus* without being reminded of the graffiti scene in *Life of Brian* where Graham Chapman writes on the wall the phrase *Romanes eunt domus*, by which he intends 'Romans Go Home'. Caught by the Roman Centurion played by John Cleese, he is given a grammar lesson as to why each of the three words is wrong. 'People called Romanes they go the house' should of course be 'Romani ite domum', because as we all remember the plural of Romanus is Romani (second declension not third), go is imperative mood not indicative, and domus takes the... locative. Only the Pythons could successfully make a joke out of the niceties of Latin grammar.

Condominium (Lat. *con* = with + *dominium* = control). An American term which refers to a group of properties, usually flats, rented or owned by a group of people. In English usage the word refers to a situation where one or more states control the affairs of another state.

Diaper (Gk. *dia* = through + *aspros* = white). Another term which, although American today, was commonly used in medieval England for a kind of white linen or cotton fabric with a small diamond pattern. The material was then adopted to be used for babies' nappies.

Esquire (Lat. *scutarius* = shieldbearer). The title given to someone deemed to be a gentleman by dint of birth or education. Its origins go back to the middle ages when a gentleman warrior had a unique insignia on his shield.

Gnome (Gk. *gé* = earth + *nomos* = dweller). The bane of some gardeners, the love of others, the word gnome was invented by the medieval scholar Paracelsus to describe the most important earth spirits. They live in the earth since a single ray of sun will turn them to stone. **Goblins** are probably derived from the Greek word *kobalos* meaning a mischievous sprite.

Juvenile (Lat. *juvenis* = young). Used pejoratively by adults who forget that not only did they in their youth behave in a juvenile way, but that as adults they still behave in exactly the same way, only not in front of the children.

Lavatory (Lat. *lavare* = wash). As we have found with extensive archaeology, even in the far flung edges of the Empire, such as Hadrian's wall, the Roman toilet was an impressive place. Constantly running water washed the detritus along channels under the rows of stone benches with holes in them. It was a very communal affair and sponges were used instead of toilet paper. The word lavatory is more properly used of the bathroom rather than the WC because it is the washing, not the use of the loo, to which it refers.

Nepotism (Lat. *nepotis* = nephew or grandson). In any political society it is who you know not what you know that gets you to the top of the pile. Giving jobs to your relatives comes naturally, but the adoption of the word **nepotism** into our language has a lot to do with the medieval popes who were, of course, celibate. I don't think so! To disguise all their illegitimate sons they promoted them to positions of power and euphemistically referred to them as their 'nephews' or 'grandsons'.

Patriarch (Gk. *patria* = family + *archein* = rule). A biblical term to describe the ruler of a tribe, it finds usage in today's language as a word used to describe the chief elephant in a herd. The female equivalent 'matriarch' is formed from the Latin *mater,* mother, after a false analogy with the word patriarch, mistaking the *patri* part to mean father whereas in fact it means family.

Pram (Lat. *per* = through + *ambulare* = walk). Pram is a contraction of perambulator a device which enabled you to walk around with your baby easily and was the precursor of the now ubiquitous buggy, which is a shame because discarded pram wheels were much better for making your own go-kart.

Siesta (Lat. *sexta* = sixth + *hora* = hour). The Roman time system for the day was one of their more chaotic systems from our point of view. The first hour began at dawn but subsequent hours then varied in length. Suffice to say that by the sixth hour you had already done quite a bit of business in the forum, had a light lunch and were thinking 'this is hot, I could do with a kip.' It must have been hard for the Roman soldiers when they reached Hadrian's Wall, where the sixth hour was likely to be cold and wet.

Spouse (Lat. *sponsus* = promised). In a Roman marriage the friends of the couple to be married met at the house of the woman's father to settle the marriage contract. This contract was called a *sponsalia* and the bride was the *sponsa*, the groom *sponsus*. The Latin word is also the derivation of sponsor in the sense of someone who guarantees a gift.

Surname (Lat. *super* = above + *nomen* = name). Once the Christians had conquered the Roman Empire your christian name was everything, much as it is today. You are recognised by your Christian name and can spend years with casual acquaintances without ever knowing their surname, which is the name over and above the Christian name.

Tenant (Lat. *tenens* = holding). One who holds property. Originally the word meant someone who owned property because they had a title to it. Today it means someone who holds it from someone else who owns it.

Annus horribilis
(Lat. = terrible year)

Whether you are a Royalist or a Roundhead at heart, you couldn't but feel sorry for the Queen in 1992. During a speech in November she described the year as an 'Annus horribilis' – a truly rotten year. She was not without her reasons.

The year started with Prince Andrew's marriage breaking up. Then in March, Princess Anne's divorce from Mark Phillips became absolute. As if that isn't enough to put your life into a tailspin, the year continued with one of the nation's treasures, Windsor Castle, going up in flames; followed by Prince Charles breaking up with another of the nation's treasures, Diana. 'Oh bother' doesn't really do it justice does it?

The phrase 'Annus horribilis' is a pun on the original phrase 'Annus mirabilis', meaning a year of wonders. This was used by the poet John Dryden as the title to his epic poem that described the year 1666. The poem was a eulogy to a year that included a famous English defeat of the Dutch naval fleet and the Great Fire of London. From our perspective it may be difficult to consider the Great Fire as part of a year of wonders, but in fact, much of London was spared from the conflagration and King Charles II was very quick to announce a massive rebuilding programme, all of which Dryden felt indicated that the year had been full of wonderful things.

The 'Annus mirabilis' of Queen Elizabeth II's reign came exactly three hundred years later, with another spectacular victory over an old enemy in a part of London that had been spared from the flames. (That's Germany and Wembley, if you're in any doubt.)

The word **hospital** derives from the Latin word *hospitis* meaning 'of a host or a friend' with all the connotations of hospitality that a friend would provide. So although as patients we don't find hospitals particularly pleasant places to be, we should be comforted by the idea that they are places where your mates are looking after you.

On the whole my family has a pretty good health record, but tell them it's a high-day or a holiday and they're into hospital like a rat up a drainpipe. Either it's Boxing Day and I'm rushing my mother into the Birmingham Eye Hospital (I had to miss a Villa home game for that) or it's my fortieth birthday and instead of partying I'm off up to Chester Hospital where my brother has been rushed in with a stomach ulcer, or it's Christmas (again) and I and my brother (now fully recovered, I'm happy to say) spend large chunks of Christmas Eve, Christmas Day and Boxing Day at Hammersmith Hospital, looking after our aged aunt who is down in London for the Christmas festivities, and is suddenly 'took bad'. What's wrong with the end of April or some time in September when nothing much is going on?

You can never tell when a **crisis** (Gk. *krisis* = decision) will cause you to change your plans. So forget Christmas and we can while away the hours at Hammersmith Hospital instead. Bro and I did have a chance to take a little wander round and look at all the departments and treatments you encounter in a modern hospital. (In case you are worried, the doctors and nurses were brilliant, sorted out the problem and ensured that our aunt returned to Birmingham after the Not-Quite-So-Festive Christmas break in apple-pie order.) Meantime, here's a resumé of what we found while we were waiting.

SOME PEOPLE

Consultant (Lat. *consultare* = take advice). The Latin word has the sense of coming to a conclusion after deliberation. So your consultant will gather all the facts together, think about them and then produce an answer. The word is also widely used in the world of business.

Doctor (Lat. = teacher). In the academic world the title of doctor is given to someone who has gained a secondary degree after much teaching. By inference a medical doctor is someone who has been taught a lot and can now pass that knowledge on to his patients.

Nurse (Lat. *nutrire* = nourish). The word was originally used to describe a wet nurse, someone used by a mother who, for whatever reason, did not want to suckle her infant personally. The word gradually came to mean anyone who looked after someone else's health.

Occupational Therapist (Lat. *occupatio* = employment + Gk. *therapeia* = treatment). OTs are wonderful people (one of my best friend's wife is one so I need to get that in early). They deal with problems that have been caused by the kind of repetitive actions associated with the work place, whether physical or mental.

Paramedic (Gk. *para* = beside + Lat. *medicus* = doctor). The word is used to classify someone who works alongside a doctor but does not have the official qualification of a doctor. Needless to say, paramedics are nonetheless highly skilled professionals.

Patient (Lat. *patiens* = suffering). When you are an in-patient you are suffering from something. If you are in a bit of a queue you may still be suffering but you may have to suffer for a while in silence, i.e. patiently...

Specialist (Lat. *species* = kind, type). The Latin word *species* is a rather fundamental one to us. We use it to describe the different classes of our plants and animals and, by association, anyone who is concerned with a particular type of anything.

SOME DEPARTMENTS

Accident and Emergency (Lat. *accidere* = to happen, *emergere* = to rise up). Accidents are nobody's fault, they just happen. Emergencies are things that occur suddenly. Put the two together and you've got a recipe for disaster which the average A&E department then tries to put right.

Histopathology (Gk. *histos* = web + *pathos* = suffer + *logos* = knowledge). All of the words that begin with **histo-** refer to areas dealing with our organic **tissues,** a word which in turn comes from the Latin *texere* meaning to weave, as in textile.

Physiotherapy (Gk. *phusis* = nature + *therapeia* = treatment). The word *phusis* refers to the inborn quality of something, so the treatment of it is looking at your own particular nature, the way you are and formulating exercises that are suitable for making it better rather than using drugs.

Echocardiography (Gk. *éché* = sound + *kardia* = heart + *grapho* = write). There aren't many words that are made up of three associations but this is one of them. You may not find this department in every hospital but it is a pretty common practice: producing a read-out of the sounds that your heart makes.

Leukaemia research (Gk. *leukos* = white + *haima* = blood). The corpuscles that make up our blood were obviously classified by a wine buff since they are red or white. The red ones carry oxygen, the white ones fight infections. Leukaemia is a disease that results in an imbalance which reduces the number of red corpuscles. When I was a child it was often fatal. Happily, today many patients can be cured but much work still needs to be done.

Diabetic retinopathy (Gk. *diabaino* = go through, Lat. *retina* from *rete* = net + Gk. *pathos* = suffer). Diabetes is a disease caused by the body's inability to absorb sugar. The natural sugars that we need simply pass through the system so sufferers need to supplement their sugar intake. It is a disease that sometimes causes problems to a sufferer's vision.

Clinical pharmacology (Gk. *kliné* = bed + *pharmakeia* = using drugs). We use the word clinic for a general place of treatment and when we think of treatment we tend to think of lying down to be treated. So it's no surprise that beds are the basis of the word **clinic**. Pharmacology is simply the study of those substances that affect our minds and bodies.

Cardiology (Gk. *kardia* = heart). The heart is central to all of us which is why its image is used to portray all the things we feel most dear to us. All the words beginnning **cardio-**

refer to the heart, right up to **cardiothoracic** surgery (Gk. *thórax* = chest). Here we meet the heart and the other organs of the chest together.

Cytopathology (Gk. *kutos* = vessel). The words that begin with **cyto-** are all concerned with the cells, the things that contain our DNA. As they're so small the cytopathology unit has a lot of microscopes.

A FEW RELATED WORDS

Injection (Lat. *injectum* = thrown in). The act of introducing some kind of liquid via a syringe has never been one of my favourites. Bro's even worse. He only has to see a needle and he faints. **Syringe** itself comes from the Greek *suringos* meaning tube. The Greek word was more specifically used to refer to the tubes of Pan Pipes, a nice image to contemplate next time you have a needle stuck in your arm.

Stethoscope (Gk. *stethos* = chest + *skopos* = examination). The ubiquitous instrument of hospital doctors, the stethoscope design remains little changed from how it was when it was invented in 1816. Somehow, in its simplicity, it seems rather outdated in our hi-tech, modern, machine-filled hospitals.

Hospitals

Resus (Lat. *resuscitare* = to arouse from sleep again). I was rather surprised to see the term resuscitation reduced to Resus on the department signboards, but I suppose Resuscitation is a long word so the board for Resus is cheaper. I blame the TV programme **Casualty** (Lat. *casus* = a falling/misfortune) where everyone seems to be in Resus whether they're injured or not.

Gynaecology (Gk. *gunaikos* = of a woman). As with Resus, I was surprised to see a sign reading just Gynae. Yes I know everyone is well used to calling it 'Obs and Gynae' but it strikes me as being, well, a little bit rude somehow. The Obs part stands for **Obstetrics** (Lat. *obstetrix* = midwife), which is related to the word *stare* meaning to be present.

Infection (Lat. *infectum* = tainted), **contamination** (Lat. *contaminatus* = touched with) and **contagion** (Lat. *contagio* = a contact) are all words which have a sense of picking something up as a result of contact. Broadly speaking, these diseases fall into two main groups: the bacterial and the viral.

BACTERIAL INFECTIONS

Bacteria (Gk. *baktérion* = little stick) are microscopic organisms which group together either in bunches, **staphylococci** (Gk. *staphulé* = bunch of grapes) or in chains, **streptococci** (Gk. *strepta* = a necklace). Treatment is by **antibiotics** (Gk. *anti* = against + *biótikos* = fit for life).

Cholera (Gk. *kholera* = diarrhoea). Mainly spread by infected water and food. Can be prevented by immunisation and careful food preparation.

Tetanus (Gk. *tetanos* = straining of the muscles). It is sometimes called lockjaw because of the difficulty opening the mouth when all the muscles go into spasm. The bacteria live in rich soil and enter a wound to attack the nervous system.

Diphtheria (Gk. *diphthera* = leather). Immunisation has been successful in eradicating diphtheria, which is otherwise a very serious disease that can easily cause paralysis and heart failure. The Greek derivation refers to the accompanying inflammation of the mouth and throat which produces a grey membrane like leather.

Typhoid (Gk. *tuphos* = wrapped in mist). A fever which produces red spots on the chest and abdomen and severe intestinal irritation. The reference to mist is in the metaphorical idea of making the sufferer dull or senseless. Spread by infected water, food or dirty hands. Some people are carriers without being infected themselves. In America in the early 1900s, 'Typhoid Mary' spent a lot of her life in custody as a public danger. She had no symptoms but could infect people. She chose the right profession to do it – she was a cook!

Dysentery (Gk. *dus* = unlucky + *entera* = bowels). Infection is usually from water or food causing fever and upset stomach. It is treated with antibiotics.

Botulism (Lat. *botulus* = sausage). A bacillus that attacks the nervous system and, like tetanus, causes paralysis. That much is clear. What is less clear is why the disease is related to sausages. The OED has it that the bacterium responsible is found in tinned food or infected sausages. Chambers, on the other hand, tells us that the bacterium responsible is shaped like a sausage. Perhaps they're both right. The word bacillus, used to describe any rod-shaped bacterium, derives from the Latin *baculus* meaning a stick.

Tuberculosis or TB (Lat. *tuberculum* = a small swelling). TB also attacks animals so it can be caught from infected milk, or from other people coughing; the bacterium is absorbed through the lungs or intestines. The disease, often associated with poverty, was greatly feared in the early 20th century when it was widespread and caused many deaths. I had one great uncle and one great aunt who died as adolescents from TB.

Meningitis (Gk. *méningos* = membrane). Inflammation of the membrane that covers the brain and spinal cord. Causes high temperature and headache and usually affects adolescents. Sadly, it can still be fatal to young children.

Anthrax (Gk. = coal or charcoal). Spread by infected sheep, cattle and horses, it can be inhaled from infected hides and can be very serious. It causes dark boils resembling lumps of coal.

ASSOCIATED WORDS

Paralysis (Gk. *paralusis* = release from control). A common symptom of both tetanus and botulism.

Diagnosis (Gk. *diagnósos* = discerning between things). Early diagnosis can be crucial in successful treatment.

Symptom (Gk. *sumptóma* = a happening). Literally what happens when you are suffering.

VIRAL INFECTIONS

A **virus** (Lat. = poison) is a simple organism much smaller than a bacterium, which multiplies quickly in living cells to cause disease. The first attack will usually give **immunity** for life (Lat. *immunita* = exemption from public office). So the greatest weapon against them is infant **inoculation** (Lat. *inoculatus* = grafted onto a bud). **Vaccination** is a particular kind of inoculation (Lat. *vacca* = cow). Vaccination involved a serum of cowpox as an inoculation against smallpox. The term is now used for any **serum** (Lat. = whey, the watery part of milk).

Polyomyelitis (Gk. *polios* = grey + *muelos* = marrow). A virus that attacks the spinal cord, resulting in paralysis. A single muscle group is affected which often results in permanent muscular weakness. Now virtually disappeared from the UK.

Influenza (Lat. *influentia* = rushing in) Severe aching, fever and catarrh. Often causes an epidemic. Not to be confused with the common cold which is mild by comparison.

Infectious diseases

Hepatitis (Gk. *hépartikos* = of the liver). Inflammation of the liver. Can lead to jaundice which appears as yellow staining in the eyes and on the skin.

Rubella (Lat. *rubellus* = reddish). Formerly known as German Measles, it gives a mild fever with a nasty rash. It is normally fairly harmless but can be serious in women in the early stages of pregnancy when it can harm the **foetus** (Lat. *fetus* = bearing young).

Shingles (Lat. *cingulum* = girdle). A painful viral inflammation of a nerve with associated skin eruptions. I had shingles in my mid-twenties. It is not life threatening but is very uncomfortable. The virus attacks a single nerve, in my case down my left arm, but more commonly around the stomach hence the Latin derivation. It is a secondary reaction to chickenpox.

Gastroenteritis (Gk. *gastér* = stomach + *entera* = bowels). If dysentery is bad then gastroenteritis is worse: an inflammation of the stomach and the intestines. It can be severely debilitating but with good care the sufferer will get better.

ASSOCIATED WORDS
With all the torment caused by the above you may want

some **sympathy** (Gk. *sumpatheia* = fellow feeling).

Inflammation (Lat. *inflammatio* = fire setting). A condition usually associated with swelling, redness and pain.

Delirium (Lat. *deliro* = to draw the furrow awry in ploughing). A disordered state of mind resulting in frenzy and things going generally awry. It can be caused by disease or substance abuse. **Delirium tremens** or the **DTs**, where it is difficult to stop your hands shaking comes from the Latin *tremens* meaning trembling, and is almost always caused by substance abuse, usually alcohol.

...a bit more than a nasty rash...

What is the difference between...

Epidemic (Gk. *epi* = among + *démos* = the people) and **Pandemic** (Gk. *pan* = all + *démos* = the people)?

The difference is quite marked. An **epidemic** occurs when there is a sudden outbreak of the same illness in a localised area. A **pandemic** is an outbreak that is seen everywhere, such as the Black Death in medieval Europe which carried off as much as one third of the whole population... and **endemic** (Gk. *en* = in + *démos* = the people) refers to something which occurs regularly but only in certain groups or areas.

The majority of words that we use to describe both household and scientific instruments derive from Greek words. At the heart of this section are the **meter**, the **graph** and the **scope**. The meters derive from *metron* meaning measure, the graphs from *grapho*, write, and the scopes from *skopos*, watcher. (These words are not repeated in the definitions.)

Anemometer (Gk. *anemos* = wind). This is an instrument which measures the strength and sometimes direction of the wind.

Hydrometer (Gk. *hudros* = water). Hydrometers measure the density of liquids. And if you thought they should be called **densitometers**, think again. These are instruments for measuring photographic density and derive from the Latin word *densitas*, meaning thickness.

Hygrometer (Gk. *hugros* = wet). Hygrometers measure humidity in the atmosphere. They come in a variety of formats and originally used strands of human hair, which have a different tension dependent on the amount of humidity in the atmosphere. **Humidity** comes from the Latin *humidus*, meaning moist.

Microscope (Gk. *mikro* = small). Magnifying glasses are mentioned by Seneca and Pliny, two first-century Roman philosophers. Microscopes began to be developed after the introduction of spectacles in the late 13th century.

Periscope (Gk. *peri* = around). Periscopes have been around for a long time and are not only found in submarines. They were used for observation in the trenches during the First World War and are used in some armoured vehicles. It is their use in submarines that makes most sense of the Greek derivation, which suggests their ability to move round a full 360°.

Telescope (Gk. *téle* = far off). A Dutchman, Hans Lippershey, is credited with inventing the telescope, but it was Galileo who famously introduced it to astronomy in 1609. He was the first person to see the moon's craters and used it to discover the four large moons of Jupiter and the rings of Saturn.

Altimeter (Lat. *altus* = high). The altimeter in an aircraft works on the principle that the air pressure decreases as the altitude increases. A sensor outside the aircraft is connected to an aneroid barometer which moves the needles on the dial of the altimeter. For most flying passengers the altimeter is something we hope the pilot will use to fly the plane safely. For some, it is the instrument that registers their admission to the mile-high club.

Thermometer (Gk. *thermos* = hot). We use them to test ourselves when we have a fever, or in the air-conditioned car to find out how hot (or cold) it is outside.

Home weather-forecasting

Air pressure is a relatively accurate indicator for predicting what the weather is likely to be in the near future. High pressure tends to bring good weather, while low pressure means it's more likely to be stormy.

The principal instrument for doing this is a **barometer** of which there are three different kinds (Gk. *baros* = pressure):

A water-filled barometer consists of a sealed glass jar half filled with water and with a narrow spout projecting upwards from the lower half of the glass jar. When the air pressure is low, the water level in the spout rises above the level of the water in the jar and vice versa for high pressure.

Mercury barometers use a tube with a reservoir of mercury at the base. High atmospheric pressure forces the mercury up the column. The measurement is transmitted mechanically to the front dial.

The third sort is an **aneroid** barometer (Gk. *a* = not + *néros* = wet). Rather than using a liquid, it uses a cell made from an alloy of berillium and copper set inside a vacuum-sealed unit. Small changes in the external air pressure cause the cell to expand or contract, which again affects the front dial.

The aneroid cell is also used in a **barograph** (Gk. *baros* = weight) which, instead of showing the pressure on a dial, writes it out. My great aunt Edith had a barograph which fascinated me as a child. It consists of a horizontal arm with a nib at right angles which draws a line on a piece of paper surrounding a very slowly revolving drum. The height of the arm is regulated by atmospheric pressure and the result is a continuous line of peaks and troughs.

Alibi
(Lat. = elsewhere.)
Plea that when an alleged event took place you were somewhere else.

If only I'd had one...

I spent my undergraduate years at Downing in Cambridge, a college that has always had an excellent reputation for Law. Several of my friends were studying the subject but it was not until my final year that I had any first-hand experience of the long arm of it. Cambridge is a city full of **bicycles** (Lat. *bis* = twice + Gk. *kuklos* = wheel). In the late 1970s, bicycle locks were either rudimentary affairs or non-existent. Most student bikes were second-hand and pretty valueless and bike theft was rife anyway. The winter of 1978–79 was particularly bitter and my friend Tim and I were forever coming out of parties to be met with a snowstorm and a long walk back to college. One evening we rolled out of a party at St John's into yet another

The Law

snowstorm and a row of bikes parked outside the college gates. Another long walk home was simply not going to happen, so it was bikes then. It did not take me long to find one that was unlocked. Tim was still fiddling with one of his many keys, trying to open a padlock, when he was accosted by a fellow student who asked him what he was doing. 'We're engineering students. We take women's bikes back to the labs, reweld the bars to turn them into men's bikes and sell them'. Typical Tim. We rode back to our rooms and went to bed.

Several days later there was a knock on my door. An **Inspector** Calls (Lat. *inspecto* = scrutinise). The details of our chat are unimportant. Suffice to say that I was arrested then and there and taken downstairs. Outside, the Inspector took a coin and scratched at the paint on a bike leaning by the doorway. 'This has recently been painted. Know anything about it?' (Yes. I found it in the college yard, resprayed it, as you can see from the paint marks on the ground just over there, and put that basket on the front where you'll find a note from my tutor which will certainly **incriminate** me (Lat. *crimina* = crimes) if you care to take a look). 'No. It's nothing to do with me'. He really should have done some more scrutinising.

The Law

To put it mildly, I was not enjoying this experience, but even in adversity, perhaps especially in adversity, you can still see the funny side of things. As I sat in the police car, the Inspector pointed to a trilby hat on the back seat.

'You can wear that if you don't want people to recognise you'. I didn't take him up on the offer. I didn't feel it would work and anyway, anonymity was the least of my concerns. Quite high on the list was the thought that I might get sent down.

Once I had made it to the police station (in full view of anyone who cared to take any notice), the desk sergeant told me to empty my pockets. As I put my hand into the pocket of my bomber jacket I felt the unmistakable cold, metal dumbell shape of a universal bike spanner. Given that this was the only object that I managed to find in any of my pockets to lay on the sergeant's desk, the impression I made was somewhat less than a sweeping declaration of **innocence** (Lat. *innocens* = harmless).

When my mind cleared slightly I got to wondering how the police had connected me to the theft of two bikes on a Saturday night, a not uncommon occurrence in Cambridge in those days. The answer was **verbosity** (Lat. *verbosus* = wordy) and **betrayal** (Lat. from *tradere* = to deliver up).

The Law

Tim's engineering lab story had made the reported theft stand out like a sore thumb from the hundred other anodyne reports of stolen bikes that crossed the Inspector's desk every day. He was convinced that he was about to crack a major criminal gang. And I was grassed up. The student who accosted Tim just happened to be the boyfriend of one of my fellow Classics students, whom I barely knew, but who remembered me being at the party and had identified me. (To be fair to her, it was her bike that Tim stole.)

We were arraigned before the **Magistrates** (Lat. *magister* = master) on the morning of 21st March 1979 and fined £30 each. (Full details appeared on page 3 of the following day's *Cambridge Evening News*.) As we walked out of court to join up with some friends, the last thing I wanted to see was my mate Duncan riding up to the court entrance on what I knew was a hot bike. 'Just to show solidarity,' he said with a knowing grin.

Advocate (Lat. *advocatus* = called to). Someone who is called on to speak on behalf of someone else.
Affidavit (Lat. = has stated on oath). A written statement confirmed on oath, that is admissable as evidence.

Bigamy (Gk. *bi* = two + *gamos* = marriage). Being married to two people at the same time.

Census (Lat. *censere* = assess). From 443 BC the Romans held a regular census every four or five years and the position of Censor was an important one.

Constable (Lat. *comes* = head groom + *stabuli* = of the stable). This is why the officers policing football grounds on horseback are never sergeants.

Decree nisi (Lat. *nisi* = unless). Divorce is an unfortunate event and when the bandwagon gets rolling the decree *nisi* is the point where the courts accept that the divorce will happen unless something else happens.

De facto (Lat. = from the fact itself). Something that stands out like a sore thumb. Universal bike spanners spring to mind.

Edict (Lat. *edictum* = something proclaimed). An order proclaimed by authority. Spoken out.

Habeas corpus (Lat. = you may have the body). The body in question is usually alive! It stops imprisonment without trial.

Incarceration (Lat. *carcer* = prison). Incarceration always sounds to me like a far worse fate than imprisonment although in reality, they are both the same. The word **prison** derives from the Latin *prenso*, a laying hold of.

This is a shortened form of *prehenso* – from which we get **prehensile**.

In flagrante delicto (Lat. = while the offence is flagrant from *flagare* = blaze). Usually a phrase associated with finding your lover in bed with someone else, but originally the flames of passion were associated with arson.

Just (Lat. *justus* = fair, right). Just refers to acting in accordance with what is morally right or proper. The word legal comes from *legis,* the Latin word for law.

Libel (Lat. *libellus* = a little book). Any kind of defamatory writing. Originally a plaintiff's statement of his case which defames the defendant. Not to be confused with slander, which is the same, only oral. Its root is the same as scandal, the Greek word *skandalon*, a snare or stumbling block.

Obiter dictum (Lat. = spoken in passing). A comment made by a judge that is incidental and has no legal authority. It may not even be about the case being tried.

Parricide (Lat. *parens* = a relative + *caedo* = kill). *Parens* is a general word for family, not parent. When it comes to killing your relatives you can be much more specific. **Patricide** (father), **matricide** (mother), **fratricide** (brother) and **sororocide** (sister). **Suicide**, of course, is to kill yourself (Lat. *suus* = self).

Posse (Lat. = to be able to). A body of men armed with legal authority. Very different from a lynching, named after Captain W Lynch of Virginia in 1780, which was an illegal court that operated summary execution.

Prima facie (Lat. = at first sight). Evidence which immediately seems plausible.

Probate (Lat. *probatus* = proved). The probate of a will is the proving of it. You need to gain probate before you can actually execute the will. Probate is only granted after any tax due on an estate has been paid.

Sub poena (Lat. = under penalty). A writ commanding a person to appear in court, usually unwillingly, to give evidence. If the person fails to appear, they will receive a penalty of some kind.

From Shakespeare to JK Rowling, our literature owes a great debt to the Greeks and Romans. Shakespeare's early comedies were modelled on the comedy plays of the Roman dramatists Plautus and Terence. The Comedy of Errors is an adaptation of the *Menaechmi*, a play by Plautus. In more modern times the motto of Hogwarts is *Draco dormiens nunquam titillandus* – a sleeping dragon is never to be tickled.

Appendix (Lat. = an addition). Both literary and medical.

Addendum (Lat. = something to be added). Another Latin gerundive that has slipped into our language unnoticed as such. The word is usually used by publishers who want to add something at the eleventh hour without disrupting the rest of the work.

Biography (Gk. *bios* = life + *grapho* = write). A book that deals with someone's life story written by someone else. Write a book about your own life and it is an autobiography, the *auto* being the Greek word for self.

Bathos (Gk. = depth). A description of writing which sees a sudden fall from the elevated to the ludicrous or pathetic. *King Lear* is a fairly good example. Deeply tragic.

Bible (Gk. *bublos* = Egyptian papyrus). Ancient civilisations learned how to use the papyrus plant to make a substance that we would equate with paper today. The Greek word *bublos* refers to a specific papyrus plant which grew in Egypt.

Bulletin (Lat. *bulla* = seal). A bulletin is a news update and was originally used to describe a military communiqué that was sealed for privacy. Gradually, the association with privacy was lost so that it now means an update on the news for public consumption.

Bucolic (Gk. *boukolos* = herdsman). A word that is used to describe a certain kind of literature which is generally poetry with a rustic theme, full of country maidens and sun-hardened labourers at one with nature. To take an artistic example, it could be used to describe the paintings of Constable but not of Turner.

Et in Arcadia ego (Lat. = and I was in paradise). The first half of Evelyn Waugh's novel, *Brideshead Revisited*, is so titled. It refers to the fact that Charles Ryder, billeted at Brideshead during the war, had been there before in much happier times.

Deus ex machina (Lat. = god from the machinery). Many ancient drama plots would reach an impasse which the human characters were unable to resolve. The standard method of sorting the whole thing out was for one of the Gods to appear and put the world to rights. As the Gods live in the sky, entry to the stage obviously requires the actor to be lowered from above. Elaborate machinery was developed to enable this to happen.

Decameron (Gk. *deka* = ten + *aimera* = days). A book by the Italian author Boccaccio which involves each of ten people telling one story per day over ten days.

Dialogue (Gk. *dialogos* = through words). Dialogue is normally used to decribe the words of a play or film. It is also used to describe the writings of the philosopher Plato that take the form of conversations between Socrates and his pupils.

Dramatis Personae (Lat. = characters of the drama). Still often seen in theatre programmes as the heading for the cast list.

Dulce et decorum est pro patria mori (Lat. = it is a sweet and glorious thing to die for one's country). Originally penned by the Roman poet Horace, the phrase was famously used by the first world war poet Wilfred Owen as the title for a poem. Where Horace meant it as an honourable ideal, Owen was using it ironically. *Dulce domum*, meaning Home Sweet Home, is the fifth chapter of *The Wind in the Willows*, in which Mole and Ratty stumble on Mole's old home.

Epigram (Gk. *epi* = on + *gramma* = a thing written). Any concise saying usually with a sarcastic meaning. It can also refer to a short poem written in the same vein. One of the shortest and most pithy was penned by Benjamin Franklin:

> Little strokes
> Fell great oaks.

Epistle (Gk. *epistolé* = send to). The *epi* in *epistolé* has a special meaning of being on the matter of something. Hence all the Epistles in the New Testament were not just communications but were making points of some significance.

Hyperbole (Gk. *huperbolé* = excess). Exaggerated statement not to be taken literally. Very much one of the devices of the Spin Doctor. The Greek word *huper* means over, so anything hyper- is excessive in some way.

Irony (Gk. *eiróneia* = pretence). Saying one thing but very much implying the opposite for the purpose of ridicule.

Legend (Lat. *legenda* = what is to be read). Legend is a gerundive meaning something that must be read. We use the word to describe a caption to something, but its meaning has changed somewhat. In the sense of myth and legend it is a story of long ago which should be read for enlightenment. By association, the heros in such stories become legendary and the word can hence be used to describe famous people today.

Letter (Lat. *littera* = letter of the alphabet). We use the word 'letter' exactly as the Romans did for A, B, C, etc. Its secondary meaning of a personal communication using lots of letters is merely a logical extension.

Library (Lat. *librarium* = a place to keep books). The earliest mention of a public library in Europe was at Athens around 350BC. The greatest library of the ancient world was at Alexandria in Egypt and was the largest collection of books ever assembled before the advent of printing.

Octavo (Lat. *octavus* = eighth). A sheet of paper folded three times to make eight sheets. A **Folio** (Lat. *folium* = leaf) is a sheet of paper folded once.

Opus (Lat. = a creative work). Used to describe any literary work. Also used in classical music, with a number, to differentiate between a composer's works. So Beethoven's 9th Symphony is described as Op. 125.

Plaudit (Lat. *plaudite* = applaud). The appeal by an actor at the end of a play for applause especially in the comedies of Terence. It is also seen in Shakespeare's play *The Tempest* which ends with Prospero saying:

'As you from crimes would pardoned be,

Let your indulgence set me free.'

Literature

Prose (Lat. *prosus* = direct). Clear and straightforward and simply the opposite of poetry or drama.

Pygmalion. In Greek myth Pygmalion was a man who would have nothing to do with women. Yet he carved a statue of a beautiful woman so perfect that he fell in love with it. To show him the error of his ways the goddess Aphrodite brought it to life so that they could live happily ever after. The story features in many adaptations, much the most famous being the stage play by GB Shaw where the arrogant Professor Higgins despises the lowly flower seller Eliza Doolittle but maintains that he can make her speak like a duchess in next to no time. As she is transformed, his view of her changes completely. It is the basis of the 1956 film *My Fair Lady*, starring Rex Harrison and Audrey Hepburn.

Satire (Lat. *satura* = full of variety). A composition ridiculing vice or folly, it was originally a hotch-potch in verse. Many poets have enjoyed the format from the Roman Juvenal to Alexander Pope, but today it is a technique more often seen in drama and journalism. It usually has a specific target such as a person, a social attitude or an institution. The long running BBC series *Have I Got News For You* is a good example.

Style (Lat. *stylus* = metal pencil for writing on wax tablets). The normal method of writing in the ancient world was to use a metal stylus to incise letters into tablets covered with a layer of firm wax. These tablets could be used over and over again so were an inexpensive way of making short notes. This brought about the first examples of handwriting and as with us, different people formed the letters in slightly different ways, developing their own way of using the stylus or their personal style.

Anthology (Gk. *anthos* = flower + *lego* = gather). An anthology is a collection of someone's favourite things and is a slight puzzle for the word specialist. This is not a true -'ology' in the sense of it being the science of flowers. The Greek word *lego* means to collect and put in order; being so similar to the word *logos* it ends up being spelt in English as **ology** because the more precise anthology is more difficult to say. So what is the science of flowers? It should logically be anthology but because this word has already been hijacked to describe compilations, most people choose from botany, horticulture or floral study.

Literature

Iambus (Gk. *iambos* = lampoon). One unstressed syllable followed by one stressed. Originally the metre used by Greek satirists. Shakespeare writes mostly in iambic pentameters with five iambic feet to the line.

> A **horse**, a **horse**, my **king**dom **for** a **horse**.

Trochee (Gk. *trokhaios* = running). One stressed syllable followed by one unstressed. Rarely found in English verse. The best example is Longfellow's *Song of Hiawatha*.

> **By** the **shore** of **Git**che **Gum**ee
>
> **By** the **shin**ing **Big**-Sea-**Wat**er

Spondee (Gk. = libations). Two stressed syllables. You can't write a proper poem in English using this metre alone, so it is always interspersed with others. It gets its name from Greek songs sung during libations – drink offerings to the gods.

In the vast majority of Latin hexameter verse such as Virgil's epic, *The Aeneid*, each line ends with a dactyl followed by a spondee.

Dactyl (Gk. *daktulos* = finger). One stressed syllable followed by two unstressed ones. Its name becomes clear if you look at your own finger, which has one long bone followed by two short ones. Much of the lyric to the Beatle's 'Lucy in the sky with diamonds' is written in dactyls.

> **Foll**ow her **down** to a **bridge** by a **foun**tain where
>
> **rock**ing horse **pe**ople eat **marsh**mallow **pies**

Anapaest (Gk. *anapaestos* = reversed). Two unstressed syllables followed by one stressed. Its name comes from it being the dactyl reversed. It is an ideal metre for use in comic verse. There are many examples such as T.S. Eliot's *Old Possum's Book of Practical Cats* and much verse by Edward Lear.

> There **was** an old **man** with a **beard**
>
> Who **said** 'it is **just** as I **feared**,
>
> Two **owls** and a **hen**,
>
> Four **larks** and a **wren**
>
> Have **all** built their **nests** in my **beard**'.

Knowing how long or heavy or bright something is seems to be naturally reassuring. We measure everything, as do most cultures. So sophisticated were the Greeks that, well over 2,000 years ago, they were able to measure the circumference of the earth to within 5% of the distance we measure today (Geometry q.v.).

Calorie (Lat. *calor* = heat). A unit of quantity of heat being the amount needed to raise one gram of water by one degree C.

Fraction (Lat. *frangere* = break). It is a vivid idea that if you break something it becomes several parts or fractions. This Latin word is also the root for **fragment** and **fragile**.

Gram (Gk. *gramma* = a small weight). We have difficulty in perceiving how much a gram weighs because it is such a small weight. Pretty good name then.

Kilo- (Gk. *khilioi* = thousand). Kilo denotes a factor of 1000 and can be used with any other base measurement. So **kilogram** is 1,000 grams, **kilometre** 1,000 metres and **kiloinch** 1,000 inches (not a measurement found in France).

Lux (Lat. = light). The way light is measured, **photometry** (Gk. *photos* = light + *metron* = measure), seems to be enormously complicated, so I'll just stick with the words.

Measurements

The standard unit is the *candela*, which, not surprisingly, is the Latin word for a **candle**. If you have one candela per square metre you have one **lumen**, Latin for the light of day. And lumens are measured in **lux**. Put it all together and you find that a candle at a distance of one foot gives off 10 lux.

Micron (Gk. = small). When we move into the world of the small we are talking tiny. A micron is one millionth of a metre. The same word is the origin of microscope, microwave etc.

Metre (Gk. *metron* = measure). About 39.37 inches. The metric scale is an easy measuring system because, like our numbers, it uses base 10. In other words it is **decimal** (Lat. *decem* = ten). The metre was originally defined by the French Academy of Sciences but the standard today is regulated by the International Bureau of Weights and Measures. Their definition of a metre is the distance travelled by light in an absolute vacuum in 1/299,792,458 of a second. How anyone can measure to that degree of accuracy is beyond me.

Therm (Gk. *thermé* = heat). A unit of heat which gas companies use as the standard measurement of usage.

Measurements

Just how long is a mile? (Lat. *milia* = thousands)

In Great Britain we still stick to the mile as our favoured unit of road distance; if it was good enough for the Romans it is good enough for us. To the Roman army (and it was the army that built the roads) a mile was 1,000 paces or *milia passuum*. This equated to just over 1,600 yards rather than our statute mile of 1,760 yards.

If you have a sophisticated **pedometer** (Lat. *pedis* = foot + Gk. *metron* = measure) you could always try to pace out 1000 paces and see if you are more Roman size or standard British. The nautical mile is just over 2,000 yards because it is based on being an **arc** of one minute of the earth's circumference (Lat. *arcus* = a bow).

So when it comes to the mile it can be pretty much whatever length you fancy provided it's a reasonably long walk or swim...

Looking at the coins in our pockets and purses shows us how Latin is still a part of our daily lives. From the humble penny to the two pound piece, every one of the British coins you handle is inscribed with Latin words or abbreviated phrases.

As a youngster, I developed an interest in coins when my parents gave me a small presentation album containing a few old coins as a Christmas present.

It started me off on the hobby of **numismatics** or coin collecting (Gk. *nomismatos* = in current usage). I was only eleven years old so the way to increase my collection was to ask people at family gatherings to go through their loose change and look at the dates on the coins. If they had a penny or sixpence bearing a date that I didn't yet possess I asked if I could have it. Cheeky, but effective. I began to build up quite a comprehensive date collection of half-pennies, pennies, sixpences and shillings.

The following year my great-uncle Raymond made one of his rare visits to the UK from his home in Bermuda. He took me to one side and said, 'Your father tells me you like coin collecting'. He presented me with a paper cylinder containing eight half-crowns, straight from the bank.

I avidly tore off the paper casing and set about looking at

the date on each coin. I was somewhat disappointed to see that every one was dated 1969, before it gradually dawned on me that this was his humourous, and very generous, way of simply giving me a present of money.

Coin (Lat. *cuneus* = wedge). The usual method of minting today is to cut out a blank piece of metal and then stamp it in a press to create the images on both sides. This was also the way the Romans made their coins, by hammering a blank wedge of metal with stamps.

Currency (Lat. *currere* = run or be current). The word currency is closely related to the word current. It is very much the stuff of today.

Decus et tutamen (Lat. = an honour and a safeguard). The motto inscribed around the milled rim of the one pound coin. Another motto that still appears on one pound coins is *Nemo me impune lacessit* – no-one provokes me and gets away with it, which is the motto of the Order of the Thistle. The coin was introduced in 1983. Its predecessor, the gold sovereign, was first struck in 1489.

L.s.d. (Lat. = *libri, sestertii, denarii*). The pre-decimal currency in the UK was a system that used pounds, shillings and pence. A pound was worth twenty shillings and a shilling was worth twelve pence. The system's written format comprised three columns headed 'L' for pounds, 's' for shillings and 'd' for pence, being the Latin words *librum* (actually a pound weight), plus *sestertius* and *denarius*, which were two Roman coins. This turns out to be an inaccurate analogy since the *denarius* (in this system the word for the smallest value coin) was actually worth more than the *sestertius* and not the other way round.

Mint (Lat. *moneta* = money). The word refers both to the practice of making money and to the place where it is made. Some of the Roman gods and goddesses presided over several different topics. One of these was Juno who in general was the protector and counsellor of Rome. In her guise of 'Juno Moneta' (Juno who warns) she protected the finances of the Empire and money was coined in her temple on the Capitoline Hill, which was called the 'Moneta', hence mint.

Obverse (Lat. *obversus* = turned towards). The side of the coin that bears the monarch's head. In our modern currency it is also the side that usually bears the date.

Pecuniary (Lat. *pecus* = cattle). Without coinage, currency will be anything that the society values. Cattle have been used by many societies to create a standard for bartering.

Reverse (Lat. *reversus* = turned around). The side of the coin that bears the design and the denomination or value. In older coins this tends to be the side that bears the date. In our modern currency only the twenty pence piece has the date on the reverse. But these things change over time.

Abbreviations on British coins

In the reign of George II his coins bore the legend: *Georgius II Dei Gratia*, meaning George the Second by the grace of God. By the time of Victoria this had developed into *Victoria Dei Gratia Britt. Regina F. D.* The section *Britt. Regina* in full is *Brittaniarum Regina* or Queen of the Britons and *F. D.* stands for *Fidei Defensor*, meaning Defender of the Faith, an echo back to the days of Henry VIII and the schism with the Roman Church that created the Church of England. In the latter days of her reign *Ind. Imp.* was added to Victoria's coins, standing for *Indiae Imperator*, Empress of India.

When Edward VII came to the throne, an interesting addition appeared into what was already something of a mouthful. *Eduardus VII Dei. Gra. Britt. Omn. Rex Fid. Def. Ind. Imp.* As Edward was a *Rex* rather than a *Regina* there was a bit of extra space which was filled with the letters *Omn.* standing for *Omnium*. Edward was now King of all the Britons. Quite which ones Victoria had not been Queen of remains a mystery.

Today the inscription on our coins reads:

Elizabeth II *D.G. Reg. F.D.* – *Dei Gratia Regina Fidei Defensor* or Elizabeth the Second, by the grace of God, Queen, Defender of the Faith.

And on the slightly wackier side..

Oliver Cromwell, whose rise to prominence owed much to his military brilliance, minted coins with the legend: *Pax quaeritur bello* = Peace is sought through war, while Restoration King, Charles II, used the motto *Dirige deus gressus meos* = May the Lord direct my steps – (presumably straight towards Nell Gwynne's bedroom).

Hundreds of educational establishments and other organisations in the UK have mottoes in Latin. This is a purely arbitrary selection (Lat. *arbitri = of a judge)*.

Aberdeen University – *Initium sapientiae timor Domini* – Fear of the Lord is the beginning of wisdom

Cambridge University – *Hinc lucem et pocula sacra* –From here issue light and the sacred draughts of wisdom

City of London – *Domine dirige nos* –Lead us Lord

Dartmouth College – *Vox clamans in deserto* –A voice crying in the wilderness

Downing College, Cambridge – *Quaerere verum* –Seek the truth

Durham University – *Fundamenta eius super montibus sanctis* –Her foundations are set upon the holy hills

Eton College – *Floreat Etona* – Let Eton flourish

Harrow School –*Stet fortuna domus* – Let the fortunate house stand

King Edward VI School, Birmingham – *Domine salvum fac regem* – Lord, keep the king safe

Leicester University –*Ut vitam habeant* –Let them have life

Loughborough College – *Veritate, scientia, labore* – With truth, wisdom and hard work

LSE – *Rerum cognoscere causas* –To know the causes of things

Merchant Taylor School –*Concordia parvae res crescunt* – Small things grow through harmony

Oxford University – *Dominus illuminatio meo* – God is my light

RAF – *Per ardua ad astra* – Through adversity to the stars

Royal College of Surgeons – *Consilio manuque* – By advice and by hand

Royal College of Anaesthetists –*Divinum sedare dolorem* – It is divine to alleviate pain

Royal Army Medical Corps – *In arduis fidelis* – Faithful in adversity

University College Dublin – *Ad astra* – To the stars

University of Sheffield – *Disce doce* – Learn and teach

Winchester College – *Aut disce aut discede* – Learn or leave

The Wine Guild of England – *Gustibus mens dat incrementum* – Knowledge enhances sensory perception

Twenty of the US states have mottoes in Latin or Greek. The USA itself uses two mottoes, the legend below the crest is 'In God We Trust' and on the crest itself a Latin motto *E pluribus unum* meaning 'One from many'. Lest we pass over Canada, its motto is *A mari usque ad marem* 'From sea to sea'. The following are all Latin except that of California, which is Greek.

Arizona – *Diat Deus* –God enriches

Alabama – *Audemus jura nostra defendere* – We dare to defend our rights

Arkansas – *Regnat populus* – The people rule

California – *Eureka* – I have found it

Colorado – *Nil sine numine* – Nothing without divinity

Connecticut – *Qui transtulit sustinet* – He who transplanted still sustains

Idaho – *Esto perpetua* – Let it be forever

Kansas – *Ad astra per aspera* – To the stars through difficulties

Maine – *Dirigo* – I lead

Massachusetts – *Ense petit placidam sub libertate quietam* – By the sword we seek peace under liberty

Michigan – *Si quaeris peninsulam amoenam circumspice* – If you seek a pleasant peninsular look around you

Mississipi – *Virtute et armis* – By valour and arms

Missouri *Salus populi suprema lex esto* – Let the safety of the people be the supreme law

New Mexico – *Crescit eundo* – It grows as it goes

New York – *Excelsior* – Ever upward

North Carolina – *Esse quam videre* – To be, rather than to appear

Oklahoma - *Labor omnia vincit* - Work conquers all

The difference in spelling of certain words either side of the Atlantic is a cause of constant annoyance to some. Center or centre? Aluminum or aluminium? Labor or labour? It is interesting to note that the American spelling, labor, is exactly the same as the Latin word, whereas over the years British has added a redundant u.

Oregon – *Alis volat propriis* – She flies with her own wings

South Carolina – *Dum spiro spero* – While I breathe I hope

Virginia – *Sic semper tyrannis* – Thus always to tyrants

West Virginia – *Montanii semper liberi* – Mountaineers are always free

The word **music** is derived from the Greek *mousiké* meaning 'of the muse'. The nine muses were the goddesses associated with the sciences and liberal arts. The muse of music itself was Polyhymnia who was also the muse of dance.

The **guitar** has been the great icon of the beat generations in its many forms: Paul McCartney playing left-handed, The Who smashing theirs up, or the likes of Eric Clapton and John Williams demonstrating technique that defies belief. It seems strangely appropriate that its origins, far from being in the swinging Sixties, are in the swinging 6th century BC. Pop icon to us, pop icon to the ancient Greeks. The *kithara*, from which the guitar gets its name, was also their preferred instrument of public performance. It was a box covered with goatskin and fitted with a crossbar to carry the strings. It may not have had the beautiful curves of the modern guitar, but see one and you would immediately recognise what it was. There are plenty of representations in ancient Greek art, particularly on decorated pottery.

Chord (Gk. *khordé* = cat-gut). Originally used to describe the strings of instruments like the *kithara* that when strummed together produce a harmonic chord.

Lyre (Gk. *lura*). The lyre was a mini version of the *kithara*. It was a soundbox made out of a tortoise shell with hide stretched over it and was played with a plectrum. The word *lurikos* meant singing to the lyre, which we have inherited as **lyrics** to describe the words of songs.

Orchestra is the word the Greeks used to describe the area in front of the stage where the Chorus danced. Its modern meaning for a company of musicians comes via ballet and opera, since the musicians sit in the area that the Greeks called the *orchestra,* and by association the name has stuck.

Plectrum (Gk. *plektron* = spear point). The plectrum has obviously had the same shape, that of a spear tip, for at least twenty-six centuries and probably much longer.

Scale (Lat. *climare* = climb). The bane of all budding instrument players is to learn to play scales, the rising sequence of notes which make up the principal chords of the different major and minor keys. They are not unpleasant to listen to since they are **harmonious** (Gk. *harmonia* = a joint). The Greek word leads to our modern connotation via the idea that a joint is where there is a perfect joining together.

Xylophone (Gk. *xylon* = wood + *phóné* = sound). As a popular children's toy, the xylophone is often made of a few slats of tin, but to be authentic the professional instrument should always be made of wood.

In the infamous *Blackadder III* episode featuring Dr Johnson's dictionary, Edmund tells the good Doctor that his great tome will only be used by people to look up rude words. So in tribute to the great man it is only right that this book should have a similar section to be glossed over by the prim and devoured by the **prurient** (Lat. *pruriens* = itching).

A tail of the unexpected

Penis (Lat. *pendere* = hang down). This is a word which is not as straightforward as it should be. The hanging down reference is pretty obvious, the surprise is that the Romans used the word more often to describe an animal's tail, rather than the male **member** (Lat. *membrum* = limb). The Greeks were more upfront. Their word for penis was *peos*, but they are also responsible for **phallus** (Gk. *phallos*), used specifically to describe the erect penis. So what word did the Romans use day-to-day? I suspect that the answer is to be found in the barrack rooms of the army where your average legionary would have used a military term for his own hanging down bit. My guess is that he may well have used the word *gladius* (Lat. = sword). See vagina.

Aphrodisiac (Gk. *aphrodisiakos* = relating to Aphrodite). The goddess Aphrodite represented an array of qualities.

The naughty bits

She combined seductive charm, the need to procreate and sexual experience in general. Her cult extended widely across Greece. It was customary for girls about to marry to sacrifice to Aphrodite in the hope that their union would produce children.

Vagina (Lat. = sword holder). It is not surprising that the word for the girl's naughty bit comes from the barrack rooms of the Roman army. The Roman short sword was an instrument for decisive action rather than pussy-footing around and could mean the difference between life and death. Naturally, the place where it was housed would also be an item of importance to the soldier.

Erotic (Gk. *eros* = the God of love). 'Erotica is simply high class pornography; better produced, better conceived, better executed, better packaged, designed for a better class of consumer.' Andrea Dworkin, American Feminist writer.

Prostitute. Prostitution has been called the oldest profession in the world although I hazard a guess that some professional palaeolithic flint tool makers might have begged to differ. Suffice to say that there have always been people prepared to offer their favours in return for some sort of reward. The word derives from the Latin *prostituta*, offered for sale.

The Greeks and Romans were capable of creating the most magnificent buildings and performing superhuman feats of engineering. More astonishing than all these great achievements is that they did it all without numbers. They had no kind of written numerical system that could be used for **arithmetic** (Gk. *arithmétikos* = art of counting). The numbers we use today are an Arabic invention. The Greeks and Romans both used letters to represent numbers. This was fine for inscriptions but virtually useless if you want to work anything out. Yet it is the durability of Roman inscriptions that is responsible for us using their notation to this day in the modern equivalent of inscriptions on our TV screens – the copyright signature at the bottom of all BBC screen credits.

The Roman numbering system uses letters to represent numbers: **I**=1, **V**=5, **X**=10, **L**=50, **C**=100, **D**=500, **M**=1000. Originally the system used a notation that added characters from left to right so that **IIIV**=eight and **XXXXXXI**=61. Gradually, a subtractive system was developed to shorten the length of the numbers (marble and granite were expensive so space was at a premium). In the subtractive system you need to take note of neighbouring number letters that are not the same. If the lesser number is on the right it is added, if it is on the left it is subtracted.

So you read **VI** as five plus one = six; you read **IV** as one fewer than five = four. Similarly, **LX** is 60 and **XL** is 40.

We never adopted the Roman notation for our arithmetic but we have taken over plenty of their words for describing things numerical.

The **abacus** bestrides both cultures. The Greek word *abakos* meant a drawing board, the sort that may have enabled Pythagoras to create his theory for right-angled triangles.

By the time we reach the Roman period (much more practical people) the abacus had become a rudimentary calculator, using pebbles on horizontal bars that could be moved into different positions. It is the Latin word for one of those pebbles, *calculus*, that has given us the word **calculate** and hence the **ubiquitous** (Lat. *ubique* = everywhere) **calculator**, as well as differential and integral **calculus** themselves.

Of course, we now live in a digital world and use a **decimal** (Lat. *decem* = ten) numbering system. These two words, digital and decimal, are inextricably linked. To see why, just hold out both hands in front of you and count your

digitals (Lat. *digitus* = finger). You have ten and this is why we count in base 10, or decimal, because counting on your fingers is a natural thing to do.

(While you're standing there, here's a neat trick to help you use your digits to do your nine times table easily.)

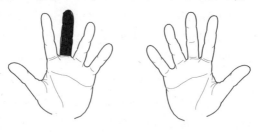

With your hands in front of you think of the number by which you want to multiply nine. In this case let's say three. Count from the left and remove finger three (either bend it down or just pretend it isn't there). Now just count out the number of digits to the left and the number of digits to the right of the missing finger, in this case two left, seven right or, to put it another way, 27. It works for all ten numbers.

Man has probably been using the decimal system since time immemorial and the Greeks and Romans used it. They simply never devised a sensible way to write it down. If we had six fingers on each hand we would undoubtedly count using base 12 not base 10. We would simply have developed two additional signs for 11 and 12. The number system behind the modern technological world works on base 2, the **binary** system (Lat. *bini* = twofold), which uses just 1 and 0. In binary notation 1111 is 15 (one in each of the increasing columns 1, 2, 4, 8). We find it difficult to operate in binary since we are used to columns which increase by a power of ten each time but are written from right to left (1000, 100, 10, 1).

There are plenty of other Greek and Latin words we use that relate to arithmetic and calculation.

Carat (Gk. *keration* = seed of the carob tree). The carat of a gemstone is the measurement of its weight; when used to describe gold it refers to the proportion of alloy metal included, with 24 carat being pure gold. Carob tree seeds were used as weights.

Kilo (Gk. *khilioi* = thousand). We use kilo all the time because it is the heart of the metric system of weights and measures from kilogram to kilometre.

Maximum (Lat. = greatest)

Minimum (Lat. = least)

Numbers

Minute and **second** (Lat. *minitus* = made small, *secundus* = second). In the calculation that divides the hour into bite-sized chunks, the minute is the first small chunk and the second is the second small chunk. Yep, it really is that simple.

Number (Lat. *numerus* = number). *Numerus* means a measure of something and is used by Roman authors to describe anything from a mass of grain to a division of the army or even your rank.

Pentagon (Gk. *pente* = five + *gonos* = angle). To us they are multiple-sided figures, to the Greeks they were multiple-angled figures – It makes no difference since the number of sides and angles is always the same. So to the Greeks a ten-sided figure was a ten angled one, a *dekagon*, which we spell with a 'c' instead of a 'k'.

Quota (Lat. = how great [a part]). The Latin word *quota* is an interrogative word like Who? or What? In this case equivalent to How much? A quota is a piece of cake. How much of the cake you get depends on all sorts of factors.

Scruple (Lat. *scrupulus* = a tiny pebble). Whenever you get a sharp pebble in your shoe it makes you feel very uncomfortable. Scrupulous people are very precise and particular so they would never put their shoes on without first checking that no such pebble was present.

The Greek and Latin words for numbers appear in a lot of English words, although some of the numbers are much more common than others.

One
Greek = *heis/hen* Latin = *unus*
Unus is common, appearing in words like **union** and **unit**. The Greek for one is only seen in obscure words like **henotheism,** which means belief in your own god without asserting that yours is the only god. **Monotheism,** the belief that there is only one true god, comes from the Greek *monos,* meaning 'only'.

Two
Greek and Latin = *duo*
Several of the number words are identical in both languages. We find them in words like **duet** and **duotone,** an illustration or photograph reproduced in two colours.

Three
Greek = *treis, tria* Latin = *tres*
The Greek stem *tri-* is responsible for a collection of words including **triceps, trident** and **tripod.**

Four

Greek = *tessares* Latin = *quattuor*

The Greek word is seen in **tessera,** the name for the small, four-sided tiles used in mosaics. The Latin word influences English through its variants *quartus* and *quadrum*. *Quartus*, a fourth, gives us **quart** and **quarter** while *quadrum*, a square, gives us all the words beginning **quad,** from the collection of four muscles around the thigh, the **quadriceps,** to the four-wheeled **quad-bike**.

Five

Greek = *pente* Latin = *quinque*

There are several instances where we see the Greek root: **Pentangle,** the 70s pop group notable for providing the signature tune for the BBC series *Take Three Girls*, **pentameter** the standard line of Shakesperean verse and the **pentathlon**. The only example of the Latin for five appears in John Masefield's poem *Cargoes*:

'**Quinquereme** of Nineveh from distant Ophir

Rowing home to haven in sunny Palestine.'

The quinquereme was an ancient galley with five rows of oars.

Six

Greek = *hex* Latin = *sex*

As we move beyond five, the larger numbers are less influential. The Greek six is seen in the word **hexameter**, the Latin six in **sextuplet**. So where does the English word **sex** come from? The Latin *sexus* means gender. This is related to the Latin *secus* meaning 'different from' as in male is different from female.

Seven

Greek = *hepta* Latin = *septem*

Neither word is common in English. Relevant words are **heptathlon** and **September**.

Eight

Greek and Latin = *octo*

Seen in the word **octet** to describe any group of eight people or things.

Nine

Greek = *ennea* Latin = *novem*

The only English derivation is **November**. The last four months of our year derive from the Latin words for seven, eight, nine and ten (Calendar q.v.). But where does the -ber suffix come from? The words come to us via French, e.g. Novembre which reflects the Frankish word *brecca* meaning 'break'. The months can be viewed as twelve breaks so we have the seventh break, eighth break, etc.

Ten

Greek = *deka* Latin = *decem*

Once we get to ten the influences increase once more. Words beginning **deca-** are all derived from Greek, such as **decagon** or **decapod,** the ten-footed crustaceans including the crabs and lobsters whose pincers are just large legs. The Latin influence is seen with words that begin **dec-** followed by an **'m'**. So **decimal** is Latin, **decade** is Greek.

Hundred

Greek = *hekaton* Latin = *centum*

The only reference to the Greek word is **hectare,** the metric unit of square measure which is equivalent to 100 'ares'. The 'are' is itself a measure of 100 square metres and comes from the Latin word *area*, a level open space. *Centum* is seen in plenty of words from **century** to **centigrade**. It is constantly being used in the term **per cent**, literally *per centum*, for every hundred.

Half-time: semi and hemi

Semis is the Latin word for the half of anything. We use it freely in all sorts of words from **semi-final** to **semi-detached**.

Hemi is the Greek equivalent which we see in **hemisphere**.

Half-time in a semi-final shows you that we just can't make up our minds which word we really prefer for the concept of splitting something down the middle. Is it a half or a semi?

The vast majority of us do a job of work that has a pretty straightforward title. This is not surprising since our society needs decorators, bricklayers, doctors, accountants and shopkeepers in abundance. However, every so often we come across people who do jobs that are slightly outside the norm and have interesting titles. These are **professional** people (Lat. *professus* = declared publicly) and definitely not **idiots**. The Greek word *idiotés* means someone who may well be very clever but who has no particular field of knowledge, in contrast to someone like a doctor. We use the word today to describe someone with no knowledge at all, which is quite different from the original Greek meaning.

Auctioneer (Lat. *auctio* = increase). The aim of this job is to keep the bids going higher and higher.
Auditor (Lat. *auditus* = hearing). Someone who tests accounts by interviewing people.
Author (Lat. *auctor* = originator). The person who originates something.
Actuary (Lat. *actuarius* = book-keeper). In insurance, someone who uses past performance to predict future probabilities.

Odd professions

Archivist (Gk. *arkheia* = public records). The ancient civilisations were great record keepers.

Courier (Lat. *currere* = run). In terms of delivery from A to B it always needs to be fast.

Detective (Lat. *detectus* = uncovered). Uncovering things leads to discovery of the truth.

Farrier (Lat. *ferrum* = iron). The connection is not with the horse, but with the horse shoe.

Governor (Lat. *gubernator* = helmsman). In a ship the man at the rudder is the boss.

Illustrator (Lat. *lustrare* = light up). A good illustrator makes something ordinary, exciting.

Interpreter (Lat. *interpretari* = explain). As the Roman empire expanded they needed linguists.

Notary (Lat. *notarius* = secretary). An official authorised to certify contracts.

Taxidermist (Gk. *taxis* = arrangment + *derma* = skin). Stuffing dead animal skins is a high art.

Odd professions

Many years ago, as a young man in Birmingham, I used to frequent a particularly lively wine bar, near the Jewellery Quarter. One evening I started chatting to a young lady sitting at the next table. Before long the conversation turned to work. Her response to my question 'So what do you do?' was a little pearl that I have secretly treasured ever since. 'I'm a **calligrapher's** gilder,' she said (Gk. *kallos* = beautiful + *grapho* = writing). What a beautiful job title, I thought. And, as she went on to explain, a beautiful job, adding gold leaf to restored manuscripts and the like.

Spend an hour in my local and you will soon understand why our language is littered today with words ending in 'ology' and words either beginning or ending with 'philia'. It's because everyone likes to think that they are either a world authority on something or want to tell you all about the subject most dear to their heart. Mine, obviously, is Villaphilia, the love of football teams in the Aston area.

The 'ologies' are all based on the Greek word *logos* which is usually translated simply as 'word'. It is the basis for the famous beginning of St John's Gospel in the New Testament 'In the beginning was the word and the word was God...' There are several nuances behind the word logos, and in the 'ologies' we tend to use it to mean the knowledge of a particular subject. There are hundreds, from **astrology,** the knowledge of the stars (Gk. *astér*) to **zoology,** the knowledge of animals (Gk. *zóion*).

There are plenty of examples throughout this book but I feel a list coming on so here are some of the less well-known ones.

bees – **apiology**	climate – **climatology**
maps – **cartology**	codes – **cryptology**
whales – **cetology**	shells – **conchology**

Ologies and Philias

cosmetics – **cosmetology**
insects – **entomology**
the afterlife – **eschatology**
cultural heritage – **ethnology**
animal behaviour – **ethology**
reasons – **etiology**
handwriting – **graphology**
reptiles – **herpetology**
horses – **hippology**
water – **hydrology**
fish – **ichthyology**
structures – **morphology**
music – **musicology**

fungi – **mycology**
ants – **myrmecology**
clouds – **nephology**
snakes – **ophiology**
ears – **otology**
rocks – **petrology**
speech – **phonology**
organisms – **physiology**
fruit – **pomology**
fire – **pyrology**
caves – **speleology**
legends – **storiology**
volcanoes – **vulcanology**

The 'philias' are all based on the Greek word *philia* meaning love of something. I have been wondering why there are fewer common 'philias' than 'ologies' and I think that when it comes to our hobbies we are more down to earth. If your particular passion is **archery,** then that is the word you will use down the pub (Lat. *arcus* = bow), although in archery circles you will probably have come across the term **toxophilia** to describe the sport (Gk. *toxon* = bow). The better known 'philias' are **philanthropy** (fellow people), **philately** (stamps) and **philosophy** (understanding). Also worth mentioning are **bibliophilia** (books), the names

Philip and **Philippa,** contractions of the Greek *ippos* (horse) and **Philadelphia,** the American city whose name means brotherly love.

Blue blood, red revolution...

One of the well known 'philias' is...
Haemophilia (Gk. = blood love)

This is a disease where the sufferer lacks sufficient blood-clotting agent and can bleed to death from minor injuries. It is a genetic disease in which women are the carriers and some of their male offspring are the sufferers. (Indeed, there have only been a handful of recorded instances of female haemophiliacs, all of whom were in families where interbreeding was rife.)

The most famous carrier of the haemophilia gene in modern history was Queen Victoria, who spread it throughout the royal families of Europe. The family worst affected were her relatives in Russia, the Romanovs, and particularly Aleksei, the son of Tsar Nicholas II.

There are some historians who have blamed the whole of the Russian revolution on the haemophilia inherited from Queen Victoria. When the initial uprising broke out in1917, Aleksei was suffering a particularly serious episode and Nicholas cared more about his son's health than about the political situation. If he had moved decisively, they say, he could have cut the revolutionaries off at the pass. The situation was probably too far gone by then but the subject makes for an interesting dinner conversation.

But whoever coined the name of the disease? Haemophiliacs hate the sight of blood because it can mean trouble. Or was it an ironic way of saying that sufferers love their blood...particularly when it stays on the inside.

...and if someone comes into the pub who says that they are a **philologist** you've got a double whammy, although a slightly confusing one. Having previously said that the 'ologies' are all about the knowledge of something, this is the one that probes the rule. Because here the *logos* reference is back to basics - a philologist is not someone who has a knowledge of love but someone who has a love of words. So probably me then.

The Olympics

The **Olympic** Games get their name from Olympia, the town in Greece where the ancient games were held. A variety of legends exist about the origins of the Olympic Games, one of which claims that they were started by Herakles. Certainly from 776 BC we know that the Games were held every four years and there are lists of victors in various events up to the third century AD. The modern Olympic Games were reborn by Pierre de Coubertin in 1896 at Athens and our modern version bears some similarities with the original Greek festival. There was an opening ceremony and oaths of allegiance by the athletes to observe the rules of the games. The first events were horse racing and the pentathlon, followed by contests in boxing, wrestling and other running races. There were also junior events for the boys. The prizes were head garlands of wild olive leaves. The first champion in the modern era was an American, James Connolly, who won the first final of the 1896 games – the triple jump. There are still various events with Greek roots – the Discus, the Marathon, the Heptathlon and the Decathlon.

Marathon (The name of a town on mainland Greece to the North East of Athens.) During the fifth century BC the Greeks were involved in an ongoing war with the Persians. In 490BC a major battle was fought at Marathon between an army from Athens and an invading army from the east. Although outnumbered, the Athenians were victorious and sent the Persians packing. A messenger, Pheidippedes, ran all the way back to Athens to relate the good news. As he reached the city he was able to say, 'We have won' before dropping down dead from exhaustion. The distance for the modern marathon was decided at the London Olympics in 1908 when the race began at Windsor Castle and finished at the Olympic Stadium. The distance was 26 miles and 385 yards. This was standardized at the 1924 games to 42,200 metres.

Pentathlon (Gk. *pente* = five + *athlon* = contest). The most sought-after prize at the Olympian Games was victory in the pentathlon, a contest that comprised five events: long jump, running, javelin, wrestling and discus (Gk. *diskos*). In the modern games men have competed in the **Decathlon** (Gk. *deka* = ten), and until the games in Moscow in 1980 women competed in the Pentathlon. This was increased at the following Olympiad in Los Angeles to the **Heptathlon** (Gk. *hepta* = seven). The first winner was Glynis Nunn of Australia.

The motto of the Olympic games: *citius, altius, fortius* means: faster, higher, stronger.

The Olympics

Pro or con?

Increasingly in the modern era the subjects of professionalism and drug abuse are hotly debated. This is something the Greeks would not have understood. Although the prizes were only olive wreaths, athletes earned big money in other ways, much like modern sports stars have sponsorship deals. Their top competitors, like Milo of Croton who won five victories as a wrestler, were true superstars. The Greeks also used quite a variety of performance-enhancing drugs. Their Olympic oath was simply to promise that they had trained faithfully and would not cheat.

If you want glasses in our village, Paul is your man. Not only does he run a successful chain of optician shops, he also has a business producing the lenses that match your **prescription** (Lat. *praescriptum* = written before). He's an exiled Brummie like myself so he must be a good egg. I asked Paul to give me the low-down on some of the words that keep cropping up in his shops.

But first of all, what's the difference between an **ophthalmic** optician and a **dispensing** optician? Two Greek words help: *ophthalmos* meaning 'eye' and *optikos* meaning 'concerned with sight'. All opticians are trying to help with your sight but it is only the ophthalmic variety that will look into your eye and do the analysis. (They are also referred to as **optometrists** or sight measurers.) So you get the prescription from them and take it to Paul, the **dispenser** (Lat. *dispensare* = weigh out), who will sort out your lenses for you.

Cataract (Gk. *kataraktés* = portcullis). A condition that leads to opaqueness in the lens and therefore to a shutting out of the outside world.

Concave (Lat. *concavus* = with a hollow) and **convex** (Lat. *convexus* = vaulted) describe the two essential lens shapes.

Cornea (Lat. *cornea* = like horn). The transparent and strong membrane that forms the front part of the eye covering the iris and the pupil. The cornea refracts light and in association with the lens helps the eye to focus.

Iris (Gk. = the rainbow goddess) the curtain, perforated by the pupil which forms the coloured part of the eye.

Myopic (Gk. *muó* = shut + *ops* = eye). Being myopic, or short-sighted, is not quite like having your eye shut but you do tend to live in a bit of haze.

Retina (Lat. *rete* = net). The retina is the network of rods and cones at the back of the eyeball that collects the light and distributes it to the optic nerve.

Spectacles (Lat. *spectaculum* = a sight). The Romans used this word as we do in both senses of a sight and a dramatic show. We adopted the word spectacle for eyeglasses in a rather romantic way that says 'when you can see properly, everything is a sight'.

Vision (Lat. *visionis* = something seen). Eyesight in its own right or a particularly pleasant view of something.

The Optician's tale

Lens (Lat. = bean). At first sight it is not obvious what the connection is between a lens and a bean. The first recorded reference to a magnifying lens was made in the 13th century by the Franciscan friar Roger Bacon.

These lenses, made in medieval Europe, consisted of two pieces of convex glass fused together. The result resembled a bean. The medieval scientists who produced them were probably monks who spoke Latin. Someone looked at the shape and said, 'that looks like a bean, that does. So let's call it by the Latin word for a bean to make it sound serious and important'. The word also gives us lentil.

Pandora's box

To say that someone is 'opening up a Pandora's box' is not dissimilar to saying that they are 'opening up a can of worms'. We use the phrase today as a metaphor to describe a decision that is liable to have unforseen and probably unwanted consequences.

It's a bit like an enlightened chairman of a golf club thinking that it might be a good idea to try and move into the twenty-first century by finally allowing women into the 19th hole. Some of the more traditionally crusty members might complain that such an act is tantamount to opening up a Pandora's box...'all Hell will be let loose'.

They really should think again. It was not the fact that Pandora was a woman that caused the problem. It was the contents of her box...

According to Greek legend, just after the beginning of time, the Gods on Mount Olympus created mankind. One of the first men, Prometheus, did the dirty on them by stealing the secret of fire. This got the Gods' backs up big time. So the chairman at Olympus, Zeus, hatched a cunning plan to get his own back. He created the first woman, Pandora, and gave her a box full of an array of lavish gifts from all the other gods. And with this he named her Pandora, which is Greek for 'all gifts'. Once down from Mount Olympus, Pandora decided to open the box and look at her treasures. Unfortunately, the box didn't contain jewels or gold, but contained all the evils which have afflicted mankind ever since: sloth, gluttony, greed, envy (pretty much the seven deadly sins, basically), which all escaped as she opened the lid.

When she realised what she had done Pandora closed the box shut. But it was too late. Mankind would forever suffer from the evils that she had unwittingly released into the world.

Yet there was one saving grace. A single gift remained inside the box. The one thing that might be mankind's saviour. Hope.

Which is what so many lady golfers, who just want to have a casual gin and tonic on a Sunday lunchtime, still have to cling to.

Like many of the Greek myths, this is a story that attempts to explain an aspect of the human condition: although our existence ought to be exquisitely happy (as is the existence of the Gods on Mount Olympus), in reality it sometimes falls a little short. Bother.

'Next thing you know, they'll be letting in people who work for a living'.

Pantheon (Gk. *pan* = all + *theon* = god)

The Pantheon in Rome is one of the most perfect structures that survives today from the age of ancient Rome. Its ceiling is constructed from an early type of lightweight concrete and forms a dome that is a perfect hemisphere. Its significance is also in what it represented, a place where all the gods the Romans believed in could be worshipped in one place.

It was built during the reign of the Emperor Hadrian, he of the Scottish wall, in AD 118 at a time when the religious sect of the people who followed Christ was becoming an increasing influence. The Christians were expounding the idea of one God as the Supreme Being, which discounted the idea that there could be many different gods. This ran counter to the Roman belief that there was a whole panoply of gods: Neptune to rule over the sea and take care of their mariners, Mars to look after their fortunes in war, Venus to help them with their love life and so on...

So was Hadrian reacting to the Christian influence by constructing a single place for the worship of all the Roman gods to counteract the growing power of the Christians' single god system? It's an intriguing thought.

Since the reign of the emperor Claudius, the Christians had been in trouble at Rome: their idea of religious belief was too alien to the Roman viewpoint. To the Romans, religion was a social activity – piety towards the gods engendered unity in society and the state.

The Romans viewed Christianity as no more than superstition; the historian Tacitus regarded it as a destructive one. Stories that Christians ate the flesh of Christ led to reports of cannibalism and other unacceptable practices. Civil unrest was in the air.

Yet the Greeks and Romans never fought wars over religion. Indeed the Greeks didn't even have a general word for religion, and the Romans accepted the local gods of the people they conquered and added them into their own pantheon of gods.

It seems that it is only when you have monotheism and the belief that your version of God is the only correct one that war starts in earnest over religion.

We use the word **anatomy** (Gr. *anatomos* = cutting up) for the dissection of the human body in operations or metaphorically in the way we describe anything's constituent parts.

Humans come in all shapes and sizes, from the **anorexic** (Gk. *anorexis* = not desiring [food]) to the **obese** (Lat. *obesum* = completely eaten) but most of us share a lot of the same body parts. People the world over have the same features of the head, for example, including a **nose**, from the Latin *nasus*. Publius Ovidius Naso, or Ovid for short, was one of the greatest Roman poets but had quite a strange *cognomen* or family name, Naso. These names were often given to branches of a family with particular traits, so we can presume that Ovid's side of the family had enormous hooters. One of the parts we rarely think about are the **tonsils** (Lat. *tonsillae*), the areas of lymphoid tissue at either side of the throat. They are part of the immune system, helping to fight off throat infections, but can quite happily be removed. Below the tonsils is the **larynx** (Gk. *larunx*), which houses the vocal chords. This is responsible both for the pitch and the volume of the voice.

The inner ear is composed of several parts. The one that does the hearing is the **cochlea** (Lat. = snail shell), so called from its coiled shape which gives it an appearance similar to a snail shell.

If you ignore the head, the arms and the legs, what is left is the **torso** (Gk. *thyrsos* = straight stem of a plant). The upper part of the torso is referred to as the **thorax**, from the Greek word meaning breastplate.

Some words remain virtually unchanged since ancient times. **Aorta** is the Greek *aorté*, **artery** is the Greek *artéria*, **cartilage** is the Latin *cartilago*, **corpuscle** comes from the Latin *corpusculum,* a small body and **vein** comes from the Latin *vena* a blood vessel.

Some words have quite off-the-wall derivations:

Duodenum (Lat. *duodeni* = in twelves). The first portion of the small intestine is so named from its length supposedly being equivalent to the breadth of 12 fingers.

Nerve (Lat. *nervus* = sinew or tendon). As the nervous system is not visible, the Greeks and Romans had a poor understanding of it. We have adopted the Greek word for tendon, *neuron*, as a word to describe a nerve cell.

Pancreas (Gk. *pan* = all + *kreas* = flesh). The gland near the stomach that secretes digestive juices into the duodenum and insulin into the blood.

Stomach (Gk. *stomachos* = throat.) Both the Greeks and the Romans used the word 'stomach' to refer to the throat.

It was only later used to apply to the stomach, probably through association with the Greek word *stoma* = mouth. The Latin word for stomach is *venter*; add *loqui*, speak, and you get a **ventriloquist**.

Trachea (Gk. *tracheia* = rough). The windpipe is made up of a series of rings of cartilage which make it feel rough on the outside.

Pastime is an odd word. It suggests that in our leisure hours we do things just to pass the time, as if we can find spare time to pass. Yet however busy our lives may be, we do still all have the odd few minutes when we can stop behaving frantically and relax.

In polls it is reliably recorded that the single biggest participation sport in the UK is angling. Given that I have spent many years working with a mad fisherman I can believe that this is true. I have a sneaking suspicion that one of the biggest closet pastimes is stamp collecting or, as it is officially called, **philately** (Gk. *philo* = love + *ateleia* = tax-free) – since postage stamps have always been free of duty. As we all love things that are tax-free we should be a nation of philatelists rather than a nation of shopkeepers, as Napoleon called us. Closely allied to stamp collecting is coin collecting or **numismatics** (Gk. *nomismatos* = current coinage). As we start taking a bit of leisure we stumble across different words for it such as **recreation** (Lat. *recreare* = to create again) i.e. you are being refreshed by a spot of **relaxing** (Lat. *relaxatio* = easing up).

Before the Playstation reared its head, one of the favourite board games was **Monopoly,** a word which derives from Greek and has nothing to do with buying up the City of London, but comes from *monos* meaning sole and *póleó* meaning to sell, hence the only seller. The connection between the two Greek words *póleó* sell and *polis* city comes from the fact that cities grew up from the economy of the market place where things are sold.

A little later came **Subbuteo,** a pun on the Latin name for the bird of prey called the Hobby. The story has been told, whether true or not, that the inventor of the game originally wanted to call it Hobby but discovered that the word Hobby was already trade-marked (obviously a trademark that never became successful) so he found a bird book, looked up the Hobby's Latin name '*Falco subbuteo*' and used that instead.

I spend a lot of time listening to the **radio** (Lat. *radius* = ray), both in **mono** (Gk. *monos* = alone) and **stereo** (Gk. *stereos* = solid), a derivation from the idea that sound coming from two points has the sensation of being more realistic, more solid. Over breakfast I am a crossword addict or **cruciverbalist** (Lat. *crux* = cross + *verbum* = word) and before going to sleep I will often read a book which makes me a **bibliophile** (Gk. *biblos* = book + *philia* = love). Good night.

For the Romans, but more especially the Greeks, **philosophy** was a big deal (Gk. *philo* + *sophos* = love of wisdom). For the Greeks philosophy meant thinking about the meaning of life, the universe and everything. For the Romans, a much more practical bunch, it was more about understanding **science** (Lat. *scientia* = knowledge), which in turn had a lot do do with learning how to build better weaponry.

A lot of the philosophical content of writers like Plato seems to be pure **semantics** from a Greek word, *sémantikos*, meaning significant in the sense of giving a sign. An associated word is **sophistry** or **sophism** from the Greek *sophisma*, meaning any cunning contrivance, so in this case a specious argument. When not arguing about words the Greeks created a number of schools of philosophy or sects where like-minded individuals would develop a particular view of the world, a moral code or set of **ethics** (Gk. *éthos* = custom or character). The names of some of these schools have been retained in our language and associated with the main tenets of their beliefs.

The **Cynics** (Gk. *kunikos* = dog-like or churlish), followers of Diogenes in the 4th century BC, developed a philosophy that we should live in accordance with nature and shun social convention. Diogenes himself made a virtue of poverty, living inside a barrel on the streets of Athens. His life was doglike in its simplicity and unconventional because he had no respect for authority. Legend has it that Alexander the Great once visited Diogenes and asked if he could do anything to help him. Diogenes' reply was, 'Yes, get out of the way. You're blocking my sunlight'.

The **Sceptics** (Gk. *skeptikos* = examined) thought that we should get away from being manacled to theories because by doing so you reduce worry and thus increase happiness.

Following on from them came the **Stoics** (Gk. *stóikos* = a colonnade) from the school set up by Zeno of Citium who taught in a colonnade in Athens. He advocated a set of principles aimed at improving moral behaviour and professing that virtue was the greatest good in life.

Other philosophies that are much later but which were named after Latin and Greek words include **hedonism** (Gk. *édoné* = pleasure), **nihilism** (Lat. *nihil* = nothing) and **pragmatism** (Gk. *pragmatos* = action).

Metaphysics (Gk. *meta* + *physika* = beyond nature) is a word that describes some of the writings of the great philosopher of the fourth century BC, Aristotle, although he never used the word himself. After his death his separate works were gathered together and published as a collection which began with the **physics**, dealing with the nature of the universe, matter, energy, space and time and was followed by the **metaphysics** which dealt with the nature of reality and events. So it was purely the order in which they appeared in the book that gave rise to the term.

Later philosophers have made Latin words famous, particularly René Descartes in his book, *Discours de la Méthode*, with his phrase on existence: *cogito ergo sum*, I think therefore I am.

Pride of place goes to Sigmund Freud for his categorisation of the **id**, **ego** and **superego** (Lat. = it, I and above I) the divisions of the **psyche** (Gk. *psuché* = soul).

The **id** refers to the unconscious which contains the drives or instincts not controlled by conscious thought, or to put it another way, **libido** (Lat. = desire).

The **ego** is the conscious mind dealing with the reality of the world around us and the **superego** is our conscience or the moral check stopping the id getting out of hand.

What is the difference between?

...**a priori** (Lat. = from things before) and
a posteriori (Lat. = from things afterwards) ..?
A priori is knowledge independent of experience e.g. all squares have four sides.
A posteriori is knowledge that is gained after experience e.g. this square is red.

Zenos' paradoxes

Some of the earlier philosophers who were trying to get to grips with the cosmos and the relationships of time and space produced some really weird stuff. And none weirder than Zeno of Elia in the 5th century BC. He is known for his **paradoxes** (Gk. *para + doxis* = alternative opinion) which aim to show that it is impossible to subdivide space and time infinitely.

One of these paradoxes describes a race between Achilles (hero of the Trojan war and thus seriously fit) and a tortoise. Achilles, being a decent chap, gives the tortoise a head start. When the race begins Achilles first has to catch up the distance between himself and the tortoise. While he is doing this the tortoise has moved forward a little so by the time that Achilles reaches the tortoise's starting point the tortoise is still ahead of him. So Achilles then needs to make up this extra distance, but while he is doing so the tortoise has again moved forward a little. This process will continue ad infinitum so Achilles can never overtake it. As this is impossible it must also be impossible to subdivide space infinitely.

A platonic relationship

A platonic relationship is used to describe one where there is great friendship but where there is no sexual activity involved. It is named after the Greek philosopher Plato one of whose doctrines was that sense is illusory but thought exists, so a non-sensual relationship is ideal. The phrase is found in a passage at the end of the **Symposium** (Gk. *sun* + *posis* = drinking together) where Plato praises the love that Socrates had for young men as something that was non-sexual and pure.

The word **phobia** comes from a Greek word *phobos* meaning fear. In Greek mythology Phobos and Deimos (another word meaning fear) were sons of the God of War, Ares. Ares' Roman equivalent is Mars, and the two moons of the planet Mars are today called Phobos and Deimos in keeping with the rather odd tradition of calling planets by Roman gods and their moons by characters from Greek mythology.

Lots of people have phobias. I know I have. With me it's wasps. Sure, no-one apart from Ray Mears actually likes wasps but my dislike is much more profound. I've got a very nice garden but at the height of the summer I'm more likely to be indoors than outside due to my **spheksophobia** (Gk. *sphéks* = wasp). (Not to be confused with **vespaphobia** which is the fear of small Italian scooters.)

I think my phobia is one that people can understand but **pogonophobia** (Gk. *pógónos* = of the beard) stretches your mind a bit further. You may not like beards but are they going to do you any harm? Clearly some people think they will.

The most extreme case I have ever come across was the phobia of one of the barmaids at my local pub. She had serious **ornithophobia** (Gk. *ornithos* = bird). I can understand that people might not enjoy being surrounded by a host of flapping pigeons in Trafalgar Square, but her phobia went much deeper than that.

On the wall of the pub is a stuffed pheasant – a beautiful-looking bird, set in a life-like pose, but very definitely dead. Stuffed. Immobile. Not in any way posing a threat. (Unlike the wasps which clearly are terrifying.) Yet she was petrified of it, wouldn't even walk past it. She realised the bird thing was getting out of control when she spent a whole weekend refusing to go into her own kitchen after her cat had deposited a dead sparrow by the dishwasher. So she decided to confront her fears and go on a course with a one-to-one **psychotherapist** (Gk. *psuché* = soul + *therapeia* = treatment). She reckoned the course would be worthwhile if it enabled her to get within a foot of the bird. At the end of the course we took the pheasant off the wall, put it on a table and asked her to touch it. After some gentle coaxing she got as far as being able to take a long brass toasting fork from the fireplace and touch the bird with that, but she couldn't bring herself to touch it with her own finger. And when she wasn't supplementing her income by being a barmaid in the pub, where did she work? She was a hands-on nurse in the A&E department of Cambridge's main hospital on a Saturday night! She could cope with the very worst in an A&E department but she couldn't bring herself to touch a stuffed bird with her own hands. Now that's what I call a phobia. Here are some more...

(Unless stated all definitions are Greek and the phobia referered to is named after the Greek word for it.)

agoraphobia (*agora* = market place) fear of open spaces.

claustrophobia (Lat. *claustrum* = a lock) fear of enclosed spaces.

trichophobia (*trikhos* = of hair) fear of hair.

phalacrophobia (*phalacros* = bald-headed) fear of becoming bald.

androphobia (*andros* = man) fear of men.

gynophobia (*guné* = woman) fear of women.

gymnophobia (*gumnos* = naked) fear of nudity.

textophobia (Lat. *textilis* = woven) fear of clothing.

gerascophobia (*gérasko* = grow old) the fear of growing old.

parthenophobia (*parthenos* = virgin) fear of young girls.

Then there is the fear of animals...

(again all the definitions are Greek and derive from the Greek word for the animal in question.)

ailurophobia cats	**bufonophobia** toads
arachnophobia spiders	**cynophobia** dogs

doraphobia animal skins
entomophobia insects
melissophobia bees
musophobia mice
myrmecophobia ants

ophidiophobia snakes
ranidaphobia frogs
selachophobia sharks
lutraphobia otters
zemmiphobia great mole rat

When you read that there is a clinical term for fear of the great mole rat you may be thinking that someone out there is having a laugh at our expense, but there are more... the fear of knees (**genuphobia**), of the colour purple (**porphyrophobia**), of the number 8 (**octophobia**), of being tickled by feathers (**pteronophobia**) and of rectums (**proctophobia**). Yes, really!

However, if you ever find yourself one night sitting at home on your own in a thunderstorm... and you're worried about being lonely (**eremophobia**) and are afraid to go to bed (**clinophobia**), because of the thunderstorm (**ceramophobia**) and the dark (**nyctophobia**), not to mention the noise (**acousticophobia**) and the fact that the date just happens to be the 13th (**triskaidekaphobia**), you can take comfort in the knowledge that there are people worse off than yourself: not just the people who suffer from **catagelophobia,** the fear of being ridiculed, but the seriously disadvantaged lot who suffer from **pantophobia** – the fear of everything!

It is only when you see a selection assembled together that you realise how many Latin (and one Greek) phrases are still in common use today.

ab initio = from the beginning. So that's where we'll start.

ad hoc = for this (purpose). It's not the best solution but it works fine in this instance.

ad. lib. an abbreviation for *ad libitum* = freely. Usually used to refer to an off-the-cuff comment.

alter ego = other I, other character. Dr Jekyl's Mr Hyde.

carpe diem = pick the day. Advice to take the best you can from the present and not worry about the future. A central theme in the film 'Dead Poets Society'.

cave canem = beware of the dog. (Just as likely, you'll want to beware of the owner!)

compos mentis = in control of the mind.

ex officio = by reason of office. In the performance of one's duties as an official.

ecce homo = here is the man. In Latin versions of St John's Gospel (19:5) this is the phrase that Pilate uses as he displays Christ wearing a crown of thorns. It has generally been used as a title for paintings depicting the scene. In May 2007 Paul McCartney won Album of the Year at the Classical

Brit Awards with *Ecce cor meum* (Here is my heart).

et al. abbreviation for *et alii* = and the others. Pretty much the same as *et cetera*.

fecit = he made it. An inscription sometimes seen on works of art alongside the name of the artist, sculptor etc.

hoi polloi Gk. = the many. The phrase is used to describe the general public in a rather sneering way. You might even say the Great Unwashed. The Latin equivalent is *plebs*.

in memoriam = in memory of. Frequently seen as an inscription on war memorials.

in situ = in place. Can be variously used to describe things being in a certain location or persons holding a certain office or position.

inter alia = among other things. Showing that the thing referred to is merely one among many.

in vitro = in glass. Most commonly used in the phrase 'in vitro fertilisation' or test tube baby. It refers to the process of fertilising an egg in glass laboratory equipment.

ipso facto = by the fact itself.

mea culpa = my fault. Part of a prayer in the Roman Catholic mass called the *Confiteor* (Lat. = I confess). People are confessing not for a particular sin but for their own human frailty in general.

magnum opus = great work. The major book, composition or other artistic work for which someone is well known.

nem. con. an abbreviation of *nemine contradicente* = with no-one opposing. Used to describe votes among clubs, societies or companies where a proposal is carried unanimously.

nil desperandum = don't panic. Things may look a little bleak right now but it will all come out in the wash.

non sequitur = does not follow. What has just been said or written does not follow logically from what went before.

pari passu = with equal step. Equally.

per annum = for the year. Describes amounts appropriate for a full year, often relating to salaries.

per capita = by heads. For each person. Often used to describe average ratios of the population, such as *per capita* incomes.

per se = in itself, intrinsically.

persona non grata = person not welcome. Such as a Blues fan up the Holte End at Villa Park.

per cent. an abbreviation of *per centum* = out of a hundred.

pro forma = for the sake of form. A pro-forma invoice is one that is sent to the customer in advance of the goods or services being provided, as a formality. It sets out what the agreed terms of the transaction will be.

pro tem. an abbreviation of *pro tempore* = for the time. A bit of a stop-gap. Something that you put in place for the time being, with every intention of having a better system in the future.

pro rata = according to the rate. Proportionately.

quid pro quo = what for what. Any decent deal has to have a bit of give and take. If you want such-and-such from me what do I get in return? Our slang word for a pound, quid, is the same Latin word.

quorum = of whom. The least number of people that a society, club or company has decided can make a decision on behalf of all the members. Literally...we have some members present of whom we request a decision.

stet = let it stand. A word used in editing to mean that a word previously crossed out should be reinstated.

sub judice = under a judge. Still being considered by a court and therefore not open to public scrutiny.

sub rosa = under the rose and *in camera* = in a room. We obviously like to do things in secret. Camera is the Latin for a chamber where business can be conducted away from the glare of publicity. The referrence to the rose in *sub rosa* is because it has long been an emblem of secrecy.

tempus fugit = time runs away. The word *fugit* actually

means flees but the phrase is usually translated as time flies. It is the name of a track on a Yes album, appears in the dialogue of the Lara Croft *Tomb Raider* film and is the title of an episode of the X-files in which time seems to disappear.

vice versa = in the position reversed. The other way round. I blame you and you blame me.

vox pop. an abbreviation for *vox populi* = voice of the people. No government can please all of the people all of the time. Every so often people want to air their views, which is why there are so many polling companies.

...and finally...

in toto = in all. Completely. That's the lot.

Most of the Greek letters are used as symbols in mathematics and physics but one of the best known is the letter π, which represents the constant relationship between the circumference of a circle and its diameter.

Roll out the barrel

For many years egyptologists were fascinated by the fact that the dimensions of the pyramids seem to have a relationship to the magical figure of pi. In 1859, a certain John Taylor pointed out that if you divide the perimeter of the pyramid of Khufu by its height you get 2pi. Then someone pointed out that the length of the sides might have been created by people rolling a barrel-like object a set number of revolutions. Given that pi is part of the relationship of a circle (in this case the barrel-like object) this would inevitably involve pi in the calculation. So there's nothing magical in it at all. Or is there?

The way that pi is calculated depends on some quite complicated algebra. The approximation of its value as twenty-two divided by seven (22/7) was first suggested by Zu Chongzhi, a Chinese mathematician in the 5th century.

Pi parties

As a rough approximation π is 22/7, which in digital money is 3.14. In a somewhat whimsical tribute to the way we denote dates differently on either side of the Atlantic, March 14th (3.14) is celebrated by scientists in America as World Pi Day and the 22nd July (22/7) is celebrated by their counterparts in Europe as Pi Approximation Day.

A byte too far

π is an irrational number which cannot be calculated precisely. A supercomputer in Tokyo did once get as far as calculating pi to two billion decimal places before its programmers gave up. (Let's face it guys, if this is an irrational number then a computer was never going to be able to work it out.) It was a fairly irrational thing to think that the computer would be able to do it in the first place.

The Romans did a lot to transform the landscape of Britain, principally, of course, creating the extensive road network which subsequent generations have been glad to develop. Their influence also remains in some of the place names they left behind, particularly in the Celtic nations.

The Roman name for Wales was *Cambria*, derivation of the **Cambrian** geological period and of the word for Wales in Welsh, **Cymru**. The Roman name for Anglesey was *Mona*, again retained in the Welsh name Ynys **Mon**.

As the Romans gradually set about trying to conquer more territory, they reached the North and Scotland which they called *Caledonia*.

The name still lives on in the title of the football club, Inverness **Caledonian** Thistle, who were responsible for one of the most memorable tabloid headlines describing their 6–0 cup defeat of Celtic: 'Super Cally go ballistic, Celtic are atrocious'. Ancient Scotland, however, proved to be one step too far. Even the Romans, who had subdued the hardmen of Europe from Romania to Spain, decided not to meddle with the Scots. By the time Hadrian became emperor in AD117 the Roman empire had stopped expanding and Hadrian set about consolidating its boundaries. In AD122 he ordered a wall to be built across the seventy-three mile stretch between the Solway Firth and the Tyne 'to separate Romans from barbarians'. Not only did it give everyone a very clear boundary point, it also served as a way of taxing goods moving between the two sides.

Once safely back in England, large settlements were beginning to grow up around the permanent army camps. The Roman army camp remains their greatest legacy in terms of place names. The Latin word for a camp was *castra*. Over the years this has come down to us in the suffix **-cester**. From Cirencester to Gloucester to Leicester, as soon as you see the -cester suffix you can be fairly sure that at some time during the Roman occupation there was an army encampment at the heart of the vicinity. Nowhere is this better seen than in **Chester**, which was the location for the main army camp in the North West.

The principal settlement in the North East was York, which the Romans called *Eboracum*. The Archbishop of York still signs himself Ebor, which is also the name for a festival of horse racing at York in August. Another important settlement in the East was **Lincoln**, which lay on Ermine Street, the great road north from London to York. Its Roman name was *Lindum Colonia*, now contracted into plain Lincoln.

In the town names of Bognor **Regis** and Lyme **Regis** the relationship with Latin is a rather later phenomenon. *Regis* means 'of the king' and simply denotes that they were places associated with the monarch. In the case of Bognor the title was bestowed on it in 1929 after King George V had spent thirteen weeks recuperating there after a serious lung operation.

An interesting oddity takes us to Cornwall and Devon in the 17th and 18th centuries. These were the great tin-mining areas of Britain and until 1752 they had their own parliament. They were known as the **Stannaries** from the Latin word for tin, *Stannum*.

The Roman invasion under the emperor Claudius began on the coast of Kent and gradually moved inland. As they made peace with local tribes, the Romans established their capital in Colchester, then a much more influential place than London. The **Thames** (Lat. *tamesis*) soon became an important waterway for supporting the military occupation and was useful in helping the expansion out of the South East. The Romans called it *Tamesis* as their best guess at what the locals called it. At Oxford the river is called Isis (also the name of Oxford's second crew in the University Boat Race) which is a contraction of *Tamesis*.

Finally, a word with Greek connections, **Triskelion** (Gk. *tri* = three + s*kelos* = leg). This is the name given to the emblem of the Isle of Man, the circular figure with three legs. It is also the emblem of Sicily.

Britain (Lat. *Britannia*). When the Romans got to the island off the northern coast of Gaul they found it a bit hard to work out what was going on. They associated place names with the names of native tribes. They had encountered the Bretons in Brittany and when they invaded Southeast England the Bretons had come to the aid of their northern comrades against the common foe of Rome. (About the only time in history that the French have ever come to our aid.) It was only after the Romans left that the French and the British got back to the normal practice of fighting each other. The name lives on in full for annual promenaders singing 'Rule Britannia' (even if, in reality, it is named after a French tribe...).

Places

Why do Hibs play in green?

Hibernia, the Roman name for Ireland, is derived from the Latin word *hibernus* meaning wintry, which was what the Roman soldiers thought about the place when they finally got there. Then, in the 18th and 19th centuries a variety of factors caused large unemployment and famine in Ireland and there was significant emigration particularly to Scotland.

The fact that Hibernian is a Scottish football team is explained by its origins being in 'Little Ireland', the Cowgate area of Edinburgh where these Irish immigrants settled and founded the football team named after their country. And that's why Hibs play in the green of Ireland.

Sporting venues have always played a big part in my life. I saw my first game at Villa Park when I was seven and spent hours as a teenager watching the cricket at Edgbaston. I've played and watched sport in a number of arenas ever since. The word **arena** is Greek for sand, reflecting the fact that the places where they enjoyed their sport were always covered with the stuff. Our modern arenas are more likely to be covered with grass or rubber matting but we still use exactly the same word to describe them.

By the time the **Colosseum** had been built in Rome in 80 AD, the word given to a stage for big events had become **stadium**. This Latin word was derived from a Greek word, *stadion*, a measure of length equivalent to a little under 200 metres. The race track at Olympia was exactly this distance long, hence the connection between the length and the word for a sporting venue.

Mention of the word **stadium** offers a handy opportunity to discuss how we form plurals of the Latin words we have adopted as our own. Should we refer to several of these things as **stadiums** or **stadia**? The confusion arises because Latin and English form their plurals in different ways. The Latin plural is *stadia*. So clearly we should we use that. Or should we? My view is very simple. We speak English, not Latin. We have adopted the word **stadium** into English and now use it as if it were an English word. So it should have an English plural formed by adding an 's'.

I've been to quite a few stadiums in my time. The most exciting? The San Siro in Milan, which is immense both in size and atmosphere, and the (Ice Hockey) Saddledome in Calgary, small but, when filled with mad Canadian fans, very exciting. And the sporting arena I'd most like to visit? The piazza in Siena to watch a running of the palio horse race – they cover the perimeter of the piazza in sand for that. Which takes us back to where we started.

Colosseum (Lat. *colossus* = giant statue). The Colosseum was named after the huge statue of the emperor Nero which stood next to it. Capable of seating around 50,000 spectators, it was used to stage all manner of public spectacles such as gladiatorial contests and wild animal fights. Below the surface was a network of tunnels and rooms.

Although severely damaged by earthquakes and stone robbers, it remains one of the finest surviving examples of Roman architecture. It is the largest **amphitheatre** ever built in the classical period (Gk. *amphi* + *theatron* = theatre on all sides).

In my local, politics with a capital P is never discussed, because it can be so divisive. Politics of the local variety is discussed endlessly. Because it can be so divisive, which at the local level makes it good sport. The Greek word *politikos* means 'relating to a citizen' and it was the idea of citizenship that was the basis of their version of **democracy** (Gk. *démokratikos* = rule by the common people).

In politics with a capital 'P' there are various levels on the political scene. At the top level we have plenty of names relating to status: **monarch** (Gk. *monos + arkhé* = lone rule), **prince** (Lat. *princeps* = chief), **emperor** (Lat. *imperator* = commander) and **dictator.** The same word in Latin and English, dictator comes from *dictare*, to read aloud.

We call the monarch **majesty** (Lat. *maiestas* = greatness) and the people of highest rank the **aristocracy** (Gk. *aristos + kratos* = best rule).

The political scene is full of **protocol,** which refers to all the rules. The word comes from two Greek words *próto* meaning first and *kolla* meaning glue. This goes back to a time when manuscripts would have a fly-sheet glued to the front containing instructions. The term is also used in computing to describe a set of rules that govern how computers communicate with each other.

In today's **society** (Lat. *socius* = companion) we are much more **cosmopolitan** (Gk. *kosmos* + *polités* = world citizen) and live in our own version of democracy where everyone has the vote or **plebiscite** (Lat. *plebs* = common people + *scitum* = decree).

Elections (Lat. *legere* = pick) choose people to represent us and from time to time we need a **referendum** (Lat. = to be carried back).

Once we have elected our **governors** (Lat. *gubernator* = helmsman) we have a group of people who can agree on everything, called the government, who have been elected on a **manifesto** (Lat. = I show clearly). There are **ministers** (Lat. = servant) and the **Chancellor** (Lat. *cancellarius* = gatekeeper).

There is then a lot of **intrigue** (Lat. *intrico* = confuse) as well as a lot of **propaganda** (Lat. = something to be spread around). Some people are **radical** (Lat. *radice* = root) while others are much more **pragmatic** (Gk. *pragmatikos* = concerned with actions). From time to time a politician will step out of line, at which point you might get an **apology** (Gk. *apologia* = speaking in defence), but probably not.

> **Candidate** (Lat. *candidatus* = clothed in white). In many cultures white is a sign of fidelity and humility. In Roman times, people who sought public office presented themselves dressed in pure white. If they were elected, their clothing would then bear a coloured trimming to show their rank.

The Latin word *Primus* means **first** and forms the roots of plenty of English words...

The first school we go to is a **primary** school where the first book we use in certain subjects is a **primer**.

In the garden the **Primrose** was so called because it is the first flower of spring, its family name being **primula**. In the media, **prime time** refers to those periods of the day when radio and TV audiences are at their peak and advertising slots are most expensive.

In studies of early life on earth the **primordial** soup filled the oceans, where changing chemistry was making the first building blocks for life. This was happening at a time which was **primeval** (the first age). Indeed anything occurring in the first stages of development is **primitive**.

Away from senses of time, the word **first** can also be used to refer to whatever is at the top of the pile...

So the higher apes, including man, are called the **primates**. In the Church of England the **primates** are the bishops while the top dog collar, the Archbishop of Canterbury, is the **Primate** of All England.

In public life the top politician is the **Prime Minister,** who may well be in the **prime** of life.

In mathematics **prime** numbers are only divisible by themselves and one.

In genealogy **primogeniture** refers to the succession of the first born, whichever sex.

In medicine a **primigravida** is a woman who is pregnant for the first time.

In law, **prima facie** evidence is your first impression of something and to be nominated as **primus inter pares** (first among equals) means that you are the senior member of a group all holding the same rank or office.

...and the **Primus** stove is a registered trademark.

An **acrostic** (Gk. *akrostikhis* = end of a line) is a cousin of an acronym, except that an acronym is just any series of initial letters.

An acrostic is a piece of wordplay
consisting of several lines of text that
read perfectly normally but which,
on closer inspection, are found to
spell out a word, or a phrase, when
the initial letters of each line are taken
in order, thus providing a neat verbal
conceit.

I encountered the finest example of an acrostic that I have ever seen when I was a young copywriter at an ad agency in the Midlands. (The acrostic demonstrated by the paragraph above is minor by comparison.) One of our clients, a shoe company, decided to take its business to another agency. These things happen, but we still had one last advertisement to create for them. Our Creative Director decided that we should go out with a bang and produced an ad with a fantastic photograph and a paragraph of text to match. The text was great selling copy, ran to eleven lines and began: 'Your perfect footwear sensation...' and continued in similar vein.

I'm sure that virtually none of the people who read the ad ever noticed, but if anyone had looked closely they would have seen that the first letter of each line taken in order spelled out what we felt about our erstwhile client: 'You bastards'. A feat, if you'll excuse the pun, of some brilliance.

Cryptogram (Gk. *krupton* = hidden + *gramma* = letter). Something written in a letter code.

Enigma (Gk. *ainigma* = allusive speaking). You're alluding to something but it's not exactly clear what.

Hieroglyph (Gk. = sacred carving). The ancient Egyptians used an ordinary written script for documents but in a religious context used carved pictures.

Labyrinth (Gk. *laburinthos*). A building with many passageways that is infernally difficult to navigate unaided. The most famous, in the palace at Knossos in Crete, gave rise to the legend of Theseus and the Minotaur.

Mystery (Gk. *musterion* = initiation). Initiation rites have been with us for centuries and are often kept very mysterious.

Rebus (Lat. = with things). A rebus is a cartoon puzzle where pictures represent a phrase in the form of a riddle. Its origin goes back to a 16th-century book of such riddles called *De rebus quae geruntur* (Lat. = concerning the things that are taking place).

For the majority of its history the language of the Christian Church was Latin with a bit of Greek thrown in. Much still remains, so this is quite a brief selection.

Apocrypha (Gk. *apokruptó* = hide away). A description of some books in the Old and New Testaments which are of doubtful authenticity. An apocryphal story is one that sounds plausible but probably never happened.

Blasphemy (Gk. *blasphémia* = slander). The Greek word was more akin to our idea of slander but was adopted by the early Church to mean slandering God.

Catholic (Gk. *kata* = in respect of + *holos* = whole). The original Christian Church wanted to appeal to everyone, even slaves – a very un-Roman thing to do. Yet by the time of the emperor Constantine it had become the adopted religion of the Roman Empire.

Conclave (Lat. *con* = with + *clavus* = key). When the cardinals elect a new pope they are locked into the annexe of the Sistine Chapel until they have done their job. This ritual was introduced to avoid events like the two-and-a-half year period in the middle ages when cardinals would not make up their minds who to elect.

Mitre (Gk. *mitra* = turban). A bishop's hat is a symbol of his rank. Given that the name derives from a word for turban, suggests a good opportunity for church unity with other faiths.

Pentateuch (Gk. *penta* = five + *teukhos* = book). First five books of the Old Testament, traditionally ascribed to Moses.

Precarious (Lat. *precarius* = obtained by prayer). Something that depends on prayers is not at all certain as is the case with anything precarious.

Presbyterean (Gk. *presbuteros* = village elder). Originally an officer managing the affairs of a local church, the term is now used to describe a form of Calvinism. Its roots in Britain go back to the Scottish reformation – Scotland's formal break with the papacy in 1560. This is an example of a **schism** (Gk. *skhizó* = split), the separation of a group owing to difference of opinion or doctrine.

Stigma (Gk. = mark made by a brand). Slaves in the ancient world were often branded by their owners. So the mark is a sign of low status. In the plural *stigmata* it refers to the marks left by the spear and nails on Christ's body at the crucifixion, which were said to have been impressed on the body of Saint Francis of Assisi, among others.

Tonsure (Lat. *tonsor* = barber). The rite of shaving the top of the head for men entering the priesthood or a monastic order. It was a symbol of the rejection of worldly goods and customs.

Urbi et Orbi (Lat. = to the City [of Rome] and to the world). This is the standard opening on papal documents and is also the blessing by the pope at Easter and Christmas.

Via dolorosa (Lat. = sorrowful road). The path Jesus walked on the way to his crucifixion.

Who knows?

Atheists and agnostics have strongly held beliefs but neither of them are at all religious. An **atheist** is someone who strongly believes that there is no god at all. An **agnostic**, on the other hand, is someone who believes that nothing is known about the existence of God one way or the other. (While at the same time admitting that he/she could be persuaded if someone came up with a really compelling case.) Obviously the real banker, if you want to get to heaven, is to choose one religion, à la Pascal, on the basis that you just might get lucky. The Atheists and the Agnostics aren't even buying the lottery ticket.

Atheist (Gk. *atheos* = not god) **Agnostic** (Gk. *agnostos* = not knowing)

Is someone trying to tell us something?

What's in a name? In the Church it's very varied, but by God, they do like their messengers.

Angel (Gk. *angelos* = messenger). An angel only has connotations of goodness by association. He, she or it is more specifically a messenger, such as the Angel Gabriel when he tells Mary she is going to have a child.

Apostle (Gk. *apostello* = send forth). Like an angel, an apostle is someone sent forth to tell the message.

Deacon (Gk. *diakonos* = messenger). A member of the third order of ministry below the levels of Bishop and Priest. Yet lo and behold when we come to the crunch he's another errand boy.

Nuncio (Lat. *nuntius* = messenger). Here we go again. Rise to a decent position in the Church and you're basically still nothing more than a bellhop, in this case the Pope's representative in another country.

Proselyte (Gk. *proseluthos* = come to). Someone who has been attracted from one creed or religion to another. By all that is natural in the world of religion this person also ends up as a messenger, proselytising their newly found cause to persuade other people to join them.

As Christianity gradually took over as the main religion of Europe, the legacy of the Greeks and Romans persisted in the titles adopted by church officials. It is interesting, when we look at the relevant words, that very few of them refer to power, but rather to position and function.

Abbot (Gk. *abbas* = father). The abbot is the leader of a monastery and a spiritual father to the monks. If the antics in *The Name of the Rose* are anything to go by he is probably their actual father, too. Abba is the word Christ uses when he calls to God from the cross.

Bishop (Gk. *episcopos* = overseer). A bishop's activity churchside is not dissimilar to that of a Managing Director layside. The sense of the Greek word is that of a person at the top looking over everyone in the **hierarchy** beneath him (Gk. *hieros* = sacred + *archein* = rule).

Cardinal (Lat. *cardinalis* = of a hinge). We use the metaphor of an outcome hingeing on a particular event which makes that event important. Next to the Pope, the cardinals are the most important ministers of the church. The same logic makes a cardinal sin right up there with the best of them.

Curate (Lat. *curatus* = cured). A curate is specifically a clergyman who has been appointed to take charge of a parish when the incumbent minister is ill or suspended, a grave situation for the parish which, on the arrival of the curate, is 'cured' from not having a vicar.

Heretic (Gk. *hairetikos* = able to choose). The Spanish Inquisition and others before them used the word heretic to mean anybody who disagreed with them. It really just means someone who follows the doctrine of their choice. So anyone who doesn't agree with your opinion is bound to be a heretic but it doesn't make them a bad person. The Spanish Inquisition was not renowned for getting the niceties right. They were renowned for surprise, fear and an almost fanatical devotion to the Pope, not to mention comfy chairs.

Parson (Lat. *persona* = mask). The principal actors in Greek and Roman drama often used a mask to represent their character in much the same way that the puppets in *Spitting Image* do. By association this leads to the idea of playing a prominent part, which a parson did in the society of his day.

Prelate (Lat. *prelatus* = carried in front). A prelate is literally someone who holds high office in the church because he has been preferred to his colleagues. It seems odd that the words prelate and prefer come from the same root. This is thanks to the most irregular of all irregular Latin verbs, the word meaning to carry. Its infinitive is *ferre*, but by the time you get to its participles it has transformed itself into *latum*.

Religious titles

Prior. This Latin word simply means former or older and is the principal office immediately below the Abbot.

Rector (Lat. = ruler). The incumbent priest in a parish, so the person who rules the roost.

Reverend (Lat. *reverendus* = worthy of being revered). This is a method of address rather than a position of office. So a Dean is addressed as Very Reverend and a Bishop as Right Reverend.

Venerable (Lat. *venerabilis* = worthy of honour). The word is used generally to describe anyone who has status due to their age or character. In the Church of England it is specifically the word used to address an Archdeacon who may be the chief deacon, but in principle he's just another messenger.

Vicar (Lat. *vicarius* = substitute). In original use a vicar was a clergyman deputising for another, usually the Rector. The word *vicarius* is also the basis for our word vice as in vice-captain who is the substitute for the captain. The kind of vice that takes one off the straight and narrow comes from the Latin *vitium* meaning depravity. And the vice on a workbench comes from *vitis,* a vine, because the shape of its winding mechanism looks like a vine stem.

Pontiff

(Lat. *pontifex* = high priest).

The word was initially used to refer to any bishop but is now exclusive to the Pope. Its origin goes back to warfare. The *pontifex* was the head of a religious order in Rome in charge of the bridges (*pontes*). The association between religion and warfare reflects the fact that bridges are vital in battle so the person who controls them is top banana.

Crossing the Rubicon

To 'Cross the Rubicon' is to do something so decisive that there is no going back. It refers to the momentous decision taken by Julius Caesar that would signal the beginning of the end of the Roman Republic in the first century BC.

At this time, Rome was trying to extend its influence over its neighbours in Europe and had developed a system of government whereby the various leading politicians of the day held office at Rome for just a single year. After this period of office, those that sought further glory were appointed as provincial governors. In 59 BC Julius Caesar had served as consul, the highest office of state. In the next year he was appointed governor of the province of Gaul, at that point only a small part of southern France and northern Italy.

Provincial governors could either sit still and grow rich on the tax fruits of their province or they could try to gain additional territory. Caesar had only one thing in mind. He raised an army and set out to conquer the whole of France. (He even had an unsuccessful pop at Britain in 54 BC.) In the end it took him a bit longer than he expected, nearly ten years in all, but by 49BC the majority of France was under the control of Rome. It was time for Caesar to return home in triumph. The correct protocol for a successful general was to disband his army outside Italy, and return to Rome for a triumphal, but essentially peaceful, parade through the capital's streets.

The north eastern border of Italy and Gaul at that time was the river Rubicon, a small river running into the Adriatic. This was the point that Caesar and his army reached on January 10th 49BC and the point at which he should have disbanded the army so that he could return to Rome in peace.

After some deliberation, he chose not to. As the Roman historian Suetonius put it, 'Jacta alea est' – the die is cast. He crossed the river Rubicon with his army still under arms and proceeded to march on Rome. Once he had crossed the Rubicon there was no turning back. Such defiance of accepted protocol was an open declaration of war on the Republic and began the final period of civil war which would eventually lead to the Republic's demise, the establishment of the Empire and the totalitarian rule of the emperors from Augustus onwards.

Decisions, decisions, decisions. You've got to make them and sometimes there's no going back, but you never know at the time where they will lead you.

People in the ancient world wanted to know what the future might hold for them just as we do. For the Greeks and Romans this kind of activity was inextricably linked with religion. Just as it was proper to **sacrifice** animals to the gods (Lat. *sacri* = holy + *facio* = make) as an offering of **humility** (Lat. *humilitas* = nearness to the ground), so it was proper to use augury, the practice of divining the future by understanding the meaning of signs in nature and in particular by looking at the entrails of sacrificed animals to determine whether the gods were looking down favourably on a person or project. The practice of augury was carried out by an **Augur** (Lat. = interpreter), a person of great importance. We use the word today in the phrase 'that doesn't augur very well...' In today's world augury has been replaced by the **Horoscope** (Gk. *hóra* = time + *skopos* = observer).

Auspices (Lat. *auspex* = an observer of birds). Good auspices are a signal of good fortune. The practice of taking the auspices probably originated with sailors who, when out of sight of land, would watch for birds to indicate landfall.

Contemplate (Lat. *con* + *templum* = with temple). In his preparations the Augur would stand looking North and divide the heavens into two halves. This area was called his *templum* and as he carefully watched he was said to contemplate.

Signs of things to come

Disaster (Gk. *dus* = unlucky + *astér* = star). For centuries any unusual heavenly body, like a comet, was believed to foretell terrible things. A well known example can be seen on the Bayeux Tapestry.

Host and **victim**. Surprisingly, these two words have similar origins, the difference between them being just a matter of size. A **host** (Lat. *hostia*) was a lamb offered for sacrifice. A larger animal such as an ox was a *victima*.

Immolate (Lat. *immolare* = sprinkle with bread). This comes from the Roman custom of sprinkling wine and breadcrumbs (*mola*) on the head of a victim to be offered in sacrifice. The parallel with the Christian Communion service is obvious.

Necromancy (Gk. *nekros* = dead + *manteia* = prophecy). The art of foretelling the future by calling on the souls of the dead. Somewhat akin to a Victorian **séance** (Lat. *sedere* = sit).

Prodigy (Lat. *prodigium* = an unnatural thing). Something which is out of the ordinary. We tend to use the word now for a youngster who is unusually gifted in some area of activity.

Sinister (Lat. *sinister* = left). In performing his divination, the Augur split the sky into left and right and anything on the left was an unlucky sign, anything on the right lucky. Several of the ancient authors suggest that this comes from the Augur's practice of facing North. The left-hand side is therefore the West where the sun sets, ending the day. A bend sinister in heraldry is an indication of a bastard.

Oracle (Lat. *oraculum* = a prophecy). In Greece and Rome there were many places where priests gave, often very cryptic, answers to questions about the future.

The most famous cryptic answer to an oracle gave rise to the tragedy of Oedipus, the legendary Greek character whose story is the backdrop to Freud's famous complex, whereby a boy makes his mother the object of his love and therefore resents his father. The word complex derives from the Latin *complexus* meaning entwined, just like the story... In return for ridding the city of Thebes from a pestilence, the citizens make Oedipus their king. In addition, he is given the hand of Jocasta, widow of the former king, Laius, who has recently been murdered. When another pestilence threatens, an oracle says that if the murderer of Laius can be thrown out of the city all will be well. Oedipus calls for the blind seer, Tiresias, who, lo and behold, names Oedipus as the culprit. Oedipus is, not surprisingly, enraged at the accusation but Jocasta points out that seers are not always right. She remembers an old oracle that said her son was destined to kill Laius and then father children with her. She has prevented this happening since years ago she abandoned her infant son in the mountains. As for Laius' death, appalling as it was, the culprits were simply robbers who attacked him in the street, at the junction where three roads meet on the way to Delphi.

This information makes Oedipus uneasy. Yep you guessed it, he has a past he would rather forget. He recalls having killed a man like Laius in the equivalent of a road-rage incident. Then a messenger arrives from Corinth to announce the death of his father, King Polybus, and to tell Oedipus that he is to become Polybus' successor. Mindful of the old prohecy, Oedipus says he will not return until his mother, Polybus' queen, is also dead, to ensure that he cannot have children by her. To calm his fears the messenger points out that Polybus was not his real father, but that he was a foundling from the house of Laius, having been abandoned in the mountains. This is confirmed by the old shepherd whom Jocasta asked to carry out the task of abandoning the boy. Realisation dawns all round. Oedipus' real parents were Laius and Jocasta. He killed his father and has had children with his mother. In horror, Jocasta hangs herself while Oedipus puts out his own eyes and exiles himself – the promised punishment for the murderer of Laius.

And according to Freud this is a normal part of a young boy's development. In your dreams!

and a sign of the times...

When Pope Paul VI died in 1978, I was learning Italian at Perugia in central Italy. That summer had been a seemingly endless succession of incredibly fine, hot days which ended abruptly one evening in early August, with the mother and father of all thunderstorms.

It was quite an event.

As I read the newspaper over breakfast the next morning I was stunned to see that the front page was emblazoned with the story that the Pope had died the previous day.

Were the two events linked? Most people would say not. The pope's death and the terrible thunderstorm happening so close together was a pure **coincidence** (Lat. *coincidentia* = occurring together).

That is probably true, but the experience did give me first hand evidence of how people throughout the ages might think that great natural phenomena are linked with higher powers sending us messages. So this is presumably why we still refer to them as Acts of God.

Signs of things to come

Perfume
(Lat. *per fumum* = from smoke)

Perfumes were first made by burning aromatic woods and gums and were used to counteract the smell of burning animals at sacrifices. Despite ugly rumours, the ancients were not into the idea of human sacrifices but loved killing a few animals, or in great public sacrifices a **hecatomb** (Gk. *ekaton* = hundred + *bous* = ox) where 100 oxen would be sacrificed in one go.

The hip bone may be connected to the thigh bone but they are more properly referred to as the pelvis and femur. Most of the other bones of the skeleton are also better known by their Greek and Latin names. The word **skeleton** itself comes from the Greek *skeletos* meaning 'dried up', since the bones were once thought of as being dead parts. The one thing we want to steer clear of is a **fracture** (Lat. *fractus* = broken up), which is the same word behind the derivation of **fraction**, a broken part of something.

The Greek word for the skull, *kranion*, gives us the alternative word **cranium**. Attached to the cranium is the jaw bone or **mandible**, from the Latin word *mandere* to chew.

One of our most vital bones is the **spine**, from a Latin word meaning 'thorn'. It is, of course, not a bone but a long chain of small bones, the **vertebrae**, from the Latin *vertere*. This word usually means turn but also has a secondary meaning of depend on since each vertebra depends on the ones above and below it in the chain.

The shoulder blade was **scapula** to the Romans, as it is to us, but the breast bone or **sternum** to which all our ribs are joined is named after the Greek word *sternon* meaning chest. Our arms are made up of three bones, the upper one called the **humerus** is the Latin word for shoulder. The two bones of the forearm are the **radius** (Lat. = spoke) and **ulna** from the Greek *ólené*, the word they used to describe the whole of the lower arm. Moving down to the nether regions we have the **pelvis** and the **coccyx**. **Pelvis** is a Latin word meaning basin, which is not a bad description of how it looks, and that funniest of English words **coccyx** comes from the Greek word *kokkux*, cuckoo, beacuse it is shaped like the bird's beak. Like the arm, the leg is made up of three bones, the **femur** – Latin for thigh, the **tibia** – Latin for shin and the **fibula**, which derives from a Latin word for a clasp since it appears to be fixed onto the tibia.

Hands and feet

Our hands and feet are a great collection of bones in three distinct areas.

The bones of the wrist are the **carpals**, after the Greek for wrist, *karpos*. The bones of the fingers are the **phalanges**, from the Greek for 'rows of infantry', an amusing way of thinking about your fingers. The bones of the palm are the **metacarpals**, *meta* being the Greek word for between.

This is all repeated in the foot where the ankle bones, the **tarsals**, come from a Greek word for the flat of the foot, while the toes, like the fingers, are also called phalanges.

The skeleton

Between these are the **metatarsals** which make up the instep, bones which were first made famous by David Beckham before the 2002 World Cup Finals.

The **solar** system (Lat. *solaris* = of the sun) encompasses all those objects which encircle our star. Most of the principal objects, the **planets** (Gk. *planein* = wander) and their **satellites** (Lat. *satellitis* = attendant) are named after characters in Greek and Roman mythology. The notable exception, of course, is our own planet: the words earth and moon are both derived from Gothic. Between the orbits of Mars and Jupiter are the **asteroids** (Gk. *astér* = star + *eidos* = form). Other rocky objects in the solar system are **meteors** and **meteorites** (Gk. *meteóros* = lofty), and **comets** with their bright, long tails (Gk. *kométés* = long haired). The best known is Halley's comet, which returns every 76 years.

Mercury	Messenger of the Roman gods.
Venus	Roman goddess of love.
Mars	Roman god of war.
Phobos	The Greek word for fear. Son of Ares, Greek god of war.
Deinos	The Greek word for terrifying. Another son of Ares.
Vesta (asteroid)	Roman goddess of the hearth.
Ceres (asteroid)	Roman goddess of agriculture.
Jupiter	The supreme god of the Romans.
Callisto	Friend of Artemis. Had a fling with Zeus. (Who didn't?)
Europa	Sister of Cadmus, raped by Zeus in the shape of a bull.
Ganymede	Cupbearer to the gods on Mount Olympus.

Io	Daughter of one of the Kings of Argos.
Saturn	Roman god of agriculture and old age.
Titan	One of an older generation of gods before the Olympians.
Uranus	The oldest god in the Greek myth of creation.
Neptune	Roman god of the sea.
Triton	Son of Poseidon (the Greek god of the sea) and Amphitrite.
Nereid	A sea-nymph.
Pluto	Roman god of the underworld.

(Listed in order of closeness to the sun. Planets in bold, satellites in italics.)

The **orbits** of the planets (Lat. *orbis* = anything round) are **ellipses** (Gk. *elleipsis* = come short) rather than perfect circles. This means that there are always two points in each orbit when the planet is closest to the sun and two when it is furthest away. These are respectively the **perihelion** (Gk *peri + helion* = near sun) and the **aphelion** (Gk. *apo + helion* = far sun). For the moon and other earth satellites the equivalents are **perigee** and **apogee** (Gk. *gé* = earth).

Spa or S. P. A.?

Sometimes delving into where words come from can land you in hot water. Spa is a case in point.

It's the one word in this book where the big guns on the jury may be out and the minnows may have a point to prove.

So here goes...

Both the *Oxford English Dictionary* and *Chambers* state that the word's derivation is the Belgian town called Spa. Obvious, but a bit lame, I think. After all, the town didn't rise to prominence as a Spa town until the 14th century and if it was going to give its name to anything these days it should be Formula 1 race tracks.

One possible explanation is that it comes from a local Belgian word 'espa' meaning fountain. I think we can count this one out if we look at why spa towns have been so popular over the centuries. It's got nothing to do with fountains.

Sure, they are places with lots of water, but it's the properties of the water that make all the difference.

The most famous spa town in Britain is Bath, where a whole industry has existed for centuries, promoting itself on the health-giving properties of the waters that rise from the local springs. I've just read Jane Austen's novel *Northanger Abbey*, where the characters are constantly 'taking the waters' in the Pump Rooms. Not unlike the way that people drink mineral water today as a healthy option.

Yet it was not in the Georgian era that Bath became a spa town. Far from it. During the Roman occupation it was a prominent centre called Aquae Sulis (Lat. = waters of the god Sul). Sul was a local British deity whom the Romans associated with one of their friendly, household goddesses, Minerva. But what does that prove? Nothing. Until...

A source of enlightenment came my way after my brother Martin returned from a conference in Rome and recounted a story he had been told on a guided tour of the Forum. His tour guide was quite sure that the origin of the word spa is Latin and is very old.

According to her it is not a single word at all, but a Latin acronym which stands for *Salus Per Aquam* meaning 'health through water'. Which sounds spot on to me.

Unfortunately the OED will only amend its entries on sight of documentary evidence. So if anyone in Bath ever unearths the wooden sign which once adorned the entrance to the popular watering hole, the Atrium SPA (your ultimate health experience with a nice glass of wine thrown in), please get in touch.

Athletics (Gk. *athlétés* = athlete). The Greeks were very competitive and the word *athlétés* comes from another word, *athlon*, which has specific connotations of being a prize for a contest as much as the contest itself.

Gym (short for **gymnasium** Gk. *gumnasion* = training-centre, from *gumnos* = naked). We join the gym to get fit. So did the Greeks, but they also went there to learn. Originally a place of exercise for soldiers in the Greek army, the *gumnasion* gradually became a centre of learning as well, ending up as the equivalent of our secondary schools with classrooms, exercise yards and extensive bathing facilities. Its name derived from the fact that a lot of the activities were performed wearing little or no clothing. This is also the root of the word **gymnastics**. The gym is a place where you might get involved in **aerobics** (Gk. *aér* = air + *bios* = life), vigorous exercise designed to improve fitness by an increased intake of oxygen.

Victor Ludorum (Lat. = winner of the games). A trophy awarded by sports clubs, schools, etc. to the year's champion. In ancient times winners of athletic events would be awarded a wreath of **laurel** (Lat. *laurus*). Today we award medals (Lat. *metallum* = metal) and in recent

Olympics, winners have been crowned with laurel wreaths as a reminder of the games' original roots.

Motor-racing is so advanced these days that all the talk is about **telemetry** and **aerodynamics**. **Telemetry** comes from the Greek for 'measuring at a distance', referring to the fact that the team controllers in the pits are constantly receiving all sorts of technical information from sensors in the cars out on the track. **Aerodynamics** comes from the Greek for 'air power', referring to how objects in motion are affected by the air they are passing through. **Formula** is a Latin word that means a rule or principle, although some of the stories that come out of Formula 1 might lead you to believe that some teams don't exactly follow the rules or principles to the letter.

The Beckham effect

Without knowing it, footballer David Beckham provides us with an interesting double-whammy. In 2003 he left Manchester United to join the 'galacticos' of Real Madrid. In the summer of 2007 he crossed the pond to join LA Galaxy. And the connection? Milk. The Greek word *galaktinos* means milky and is the derivation both of Real Madrid's nickname, thanks to their all-white strip, and the word 'galaxy'. The Greeks thought that the few galaxies that are visible to the naked eye looked like a fuzzy blur, almost as if they were a small drop of milk. Advanced thinking at the time, which we have copied by calling the main disc of our galaxy the Milky Way.

And finally, of course, don't forget that Galaxy is a brand of milk chocolate.

We use **symbols** all the time. The term comes from the Greek *sumbolon*, meaning a signal or token. The Greek word can even mean a beacon-fire, demonstrating that symbols are things of which we take great notice. When I start thinking about writing anything I know I'm going to be using **punctuation**. Not only is it the proper thing to do, but well-punctuated writing is both easier to read and clearer in meaning. Making sense of writing that has no punctuation can sometimes be quite tricky, which is probably why legal documents never use it: the lawyers really do want to bamboozle you! Even in text messages I at least punctuate thoughts by putting in full stops. (Probably because it's easy, knowing that it's just the No. 1 key.) The word **punctuate** is derived from the Latin *punctuare*, which means to sting or make a small point. The same word gives us **puncture** and **punctual,** through the idea that a point is a precise moment in time so there's not much leeway about arriving either side of it.

Several of the more common words for punctuation marks have Greek origins. The **apostrophe** comes from *apostrophos* meaning turned away. This refers to its usage to indicate omitted letters, e.g. can't for can not. Its other usage is to indicate possession, e.g. John's car. The commonest misuse is in the two versions of the word 'its'. On the one hand 'its' indicates possession, e.g. 'Genesis gets its name from...' On the other hand, 'it's' is a short form of it is. It might be tempting to say that both should have an apostrophe, but common usage is only to write it's when you mean it is.

Words can be separated by **commas,** deriving from a Greek word, *komma,* meaning something cut off, or **colons** and **semi-colons,** deriving from the word *kólon,* meaning part of something. Semi-colon is an example of two words joined together by a **hyphen,** which comes from the Greek *hupo + hen,* meaning bringing together as one thing.

The **asterisk** symbol comes from the Greek *asterikos,* the diminutive of *astér,* star, so it means a small star. This describes its appearance as either a five radius ★ or six radius ✳ design, resembling a twinkling star.

The double dot symbol ¨ over a vowel is often referred to by the German word umlaut. Although it is only used in words we have appropriated from other languages, we do have our own word for it – **diaeresis** from the Greek *diaireó,* to break apart. The sign indicates that the vowel in question should be pronounced separately, e.g. Brontë or naïve.

Symbols and signs

Of course, letters themselves are merely symbols and people form them in very different ways in their own handwriting.

One of my favourite subjects at university was **palaeography,** or the study of old writing. I considered it a great treat to have tutorials in the vaults of Cambridge's Fitzwilliam Museum where we were allowed to look at ancient manuscripts brought out from the museum's safes by men wearing white gloves. The manuscripts are absolutely priceless objects, very beautiful to look at but seriously difficult to read. Most were produced by monks working in the monasteries of medieval Europe. They wrote, mostly in Latin, on vellum, which was a very expensive material. To save space they not only gave up on punctuation, they also didn't use word breaks. As if this doesn't make it difficult enough to read, the standard way of writing at that time made no differentiation between the letters u, v and n, all of which look like a u, while the m looks like a double-u. As a result, a lot of the manuscripts look like a constant series of 'u's, which make them very difficult to decipher but do make a very interesting puzzle.

Symbols and signs

How the ampersand got its name

The ampersand is a common sign used as an abbreviation for the word 'and'. It is a symbol that represents a ligature of the letters 'e' and 't' which make up the Latin word *et*, which means **and**.

The symbol is found in Roman sources from the first century AD and it is generally thought to have been invented by Tiro, who, as the secretary of the great lawyer and politician Cicero, developed a form of shorthand in the first century BC.

For many years it was regarded as the last letter of the English alphabet and this is how it got its name. The word is a contraction of the phrase 'and per se and'. When children were being taught the alphabet, after 'z' the teacher would say 'and per se and' meaning 'and [the symbol that is] in itself and.'

Original versions of the ampersand (on the left) show its true ligature format joining 'e' and 't'. Over time its formation has changed so that it is no longer recognisible as the et ligature.

Archaeology (Gk. *archaios* + *logos* = knowledge of ancient things) has gained a huge public following thanks to the Channel Four programme, *Time Team*, presented by Tony Robinson and his colourful band of **experts** (Lat. *expertus* = thoroughly tested). It is an intriguing mixture whereby modern technology enables us to expose and piece together what human life was like in the past.

Most programmes begin with a full evaluation of the site, partly carried out by the geophysics team. **Geophysics** (Gk. *gé* + *phusis* = nature of the earth) uses various techniques to detect patterns below the soil surface which show up as **anomalies** (Gk *anómalos* = uneven) indicating where building foundations from old structures may be present. It is a science that has rather been championed by *Time Team* and is reverently referred to by Tony as Geofiz (I wouldn't mind betting that during production that is exactly how everyone spells it, as well).

Once they have decided on some promising **sites** (Lat. *situs* = the local position) they can begin the work of **excavation** (Lat. *ex* + *cavare* = hollow out) by putting in some **trenches** (Lat. *truncus* = cut out). The first things they hope to find are objects relating to the people who used to live there, usually called **artefacts** (Lat. *arte* + *factum* = made by skill).

Time team

These can be shards of pottery, coins, nails and personal items such as jewellery. On some sites skeletons are uncovered, the remains of our **ancestors** (Lat. *ante + cessum* = gone before). From time to time specialists are called in who can look at associated topics such as a **dendrochronology** (Gk. *dendron + chronos + logos* = knowledge of the age of trees), who can offer timing information, or a **botanist** (Gk. *botané* = grass or fodder), who can identify plants used to make fabrics or provide food. Another word that crops up regularly is **palaeontologist** (Gk. *palaios + onta + logos* = knowledge of ancient living).

Many programmes look at the Roman sites which date back to the time when Britain was part of the Roman Empire but occasionally a site will be discovered that charts an age before recorded history, looking at people living in what we now refer to as the **palaeolithic** (Gk. *palaios* = ancient + *lithos* = stone) and **neolithic** ages (Gk. *neos* = new), named after the period when stone tools were being developed and early mankind was adapting to new **technology** (Gk. *techné + logos* = knowledge of skills). Our modern equivalents would perhaps be the palaeomobile (a large brick of a phone) and the neomobile (slim enough to fit in your shirt pocket and capable of taking hi-res photos of archaeological dig sites).

Tombs

When someone has died the physical body needs to be put to rest properly. As this is something we all have to deal with in our lives, we have plenty of words that relate to the subject.

We can start by looking at the subtle difference between two Greek words, *tumbos* and *taphos*.

Tumbos referred to the place where a body was burned before a mound of soil was raised over the ashes. The Roman equivalent, the **tumulus,** comes from a Latin word meaning to swell. The ordnance survey maps of Britain show hundreds of such burial mounds.

Taphos on the other hand referred to the place of burial, the wake and all the other associated paraphernalia.

It is interesting to see how over time we have kept the words but given them different meanings. To us a **tomb** is now a place of burial rather than the place where a body is burned, which is the **crematorium** (Lat. *crematum* = burned).

The *taphos* root remains in our language in the **cenotaph,** scene of annual Remembrance Sunday ceremonies. The 'ceno' part derives from a Greek word meaning empty since it is not a true grave but a memorial sculpture, full of significance but empty of bodies. An **epitaph** originally meant a comment on a gravestone, although it is used metaphorically to describe any phrase associated with the character of someone departed.

Over the centuries, people in high places have put great store by the **monuments** that they can build as lasting memorials to their lives. The Latin word *monumentum* is derived from *monere*, 'to remind', the importance being in the memory not the scale. But when we are talking scale there is none greater than the amazing feat of Egyptian society – the great **Pyramids** built at Giza around 2500BC. The Greek word *puramidos*, which has come down to us, is probably their best estimate of the word the ancient Egyptians used for the structures.

One of the Seven Wonders of the ancient world was a tomb, the **Mausoleum** at Halicarnassus. A fantastic structure which modern excavations in Turkey have estimated as being at least 140 feet high, it was the monument of the king of Caria, Mausolus, who reigned in the fourth century BC.

For centuries in Britain the word we are most likely to associate with our dear departed is the **cemetery** and with good reason. The Greek word *koimeterion*, from which it derives, means a dormitory or sleeping place. A very peaceful thought.

Tombs

Many of the richer ancient cultures buried the bodies of their leaders in a stone coffin which generally goes by the name of **sarcophagos**. This derives from two Greek words *sarco* meaning 'flesh' and *phagein* meaning 'to eat', since it was widely believed that the stone coffin quickly consumed the flesh.

For thousands of years a human's only way of moving around on land was to put one leg in front of the other. Then along came the caveman era's own Mr Einstein with a cute little idea and, lo and behold, we had the wheel. After that little leap forward transport took off big time and the ability to move quickly over distances has fascinated us ever since.

Accelerator (Lat. *accelerare* = speed up). A simple definition which gives a very accurate description of what happens when you put your foot on the gas.

Aeroplane (Gk. *aér* = air + Lat. *planum* = flat surface). Combinations of a Greek and Latin root always indicate a word that has been coined relatively recently. The flat surface in question refers to the shape of the wing's underside.

Apollo. NASA's Apollo moon programme was named after the Greek God of healing and prophecy. Unfortunately, no one prophesied the problems encountered by Apollo 13 but the spacecraft was healed after a fashion and the astronauts were miraculously saved.

Bus (abbreviation of Lat. *omnibus* = for everyone). Bus is a shortened form of its original title, omnibus. In that guise it has for many years been used as a way to describe the man in the street, as in 'the man on the Clapham Omnibus.'

Metro (Gk. *metropolis* = mother city). Many major cities have underground systems or metros. On a wider level the idea of the metropolis is the great place where people congregate, so the sort of place that is likely to support a major train network.

Tandem (Lat. = at length). The name *tandem* is a joke on the Latin word *tandem*, meaning 'at length' to describe the oversized bicycle. Further development by seventies comedy series, *The Goodies*, saw a three-man bicycle which they called the trandem, a further joke based around the word *tri* meaning three.

Titanic. When it was launched in 1912 the Titanic was the largest movable object that had ever been built. It was named after the Titans in Greek mythology. They were a race of giants that represented the forces of nature. Unfortunately, none of them represented icebergs.

Transport. The Latin word *transportare* simply means to carry across, which is a very succinct way to describe our modern idea of transport as moving things elsewhere.

Vehicle (Lat. *vehiculum* = carrying thing). The Romans used the word in exactly the same way as we do now.

Trireme (Lat. *triremi* = three oars)

The ultimate warship devised by the Greeks and improved by the Romans, a trireme must have seemed an awesome weapon in its day, with its bronze prow being used as a battering ram on opposing ships. It was around forty metres long with three files of oarsmen on either side, one above the other. The crew comprised around 200 men using oars, the largest of which were over four metres long. The co-ordination of rowers in an eight-man boat is pretty difficult, but in a trireme the men kept their coordination to the beat of a drum. A full scale replica was launched in Greece in 1987 which demonstrated that a speed of nine knots is attainable.

The Trojan War

Homer's epic poem, *The Iliad*, comprises twenty-four books which together recount the story of the ten-year battle between the Greeks and the people of Troy, a great walled city on the coast of modern day Turkey.

There seems some credence in the idea that the story relates to a slave trade between Greece and Turkey associated particularly with **nubile** women. (The Latin word *nubilis* strictly means 'of marriageable age' and has nothing to do with looks.) What is certain is that the story forms the backdrop not only to much classical literature but also to much modern European culture.

Homer's book is a big one. Here it is in one minute...

The Trojan prince, Paris, a bit of a chancer, is invited to visit Greece as a guest of King Menelaus of Sparta. He has a wonderful holiday but his choice of souvenir to take home, his host's beautiful wife Helen, represents a serious breach of etiquette. So Menelaus and his brother Agamemnon enlist a huge army and sail to Troy with a band of heroes including Ajax, Achilles and Odysseus (hence Helen's soubriquet as the 'face that could launch a thousand ships').

Once they get there, the Greeks set up camp outside Troy and spend the next ten years besieging it to little effect.

The Trojan War

Various of the ancient gods support one side or the other and interfere interminably, which leads to all sorts of rivalries and chaos. Eventually everybody gets totally fed up and Odysseus comes up with a plan so cunning it would be worthy of Baldrick, the only difference being that this one works. He tells the Greeks to build a huge wooden horse on a wheeled platform, leave it at the gates to the city and pretend to sail away.

The Trojans think the horse is a gift; they open the gates and wheel it into the city. That night the Greeks hidden inside the body of the horse emerge and open the gates, ushering in the rest of the army who slaughter the Trojans, regain Helen and sail back home. On their return, Menelaus and Agamemnon find their kingdoms in a right bloody mess which ends up with everybody getting killed in retribution for all sorts of ills, enmities and jealousies. And you thought Hamlet was a bloodbath.

Washing up meets football

The Iliad still has its echoes in our language today. To me, as a youngster, Ajax was not a Greek hero: Ajax was a scouring powder my mother used to sprinkle over the dish that the Sunday roast had been cooked in before washing it. Then I

The Trojan War

discovered football and another great European hero. This one wasn't Greek and he wasn't called Ajax. He was Dutch, called Johann Cruyff and he played football for a team called Ajax. Funny how the Trojan War references keep cropping up.

The science of volcanoes is called **Vulcanology**, meaning knowledge of the Roman god of fire, *Volcanus*, or as we call him, **Vulcan**.

Volcanoes are **vents** (Lat. *ventus* = wind) in the earth's **crust** (Lat. *crusta* = shell) above masses of molten rock lying close to the surface. Below the volcano a chamber develops where the molten rock, called **magma**, a Greek word meaning kneaded dough, begins to build up pressure. When the pressure gets too high the volcano **erupts** (Lat. *eruptus* = broken out) will either send a plume of hot ash and gases into the air or spew down the sides of the volcano a river of **lava** (Lat. *lavare* = wash over).

If the ash does not go straight up it may rush down the sides of the volcano in a **pyroclastic** flow (Gk. *puro* + *klastos* = broken fire), referring to the fact that the ash clouds contain millions of broken fragments of hot rock and gases. These clouds of ash are superheated and move incredibly fast – this was the nature of the eruption of Mount St Helens, in Washington State in 1980.

Pieces of the ash that have fallen to earth are called **pumice** (Lat. *pumicis* = volcanic ash) which is very light and abrasive and has a variety of uses.

The hole created in the top of the volcano by the eruption

is called a **crater** (Gk. = mixing bowl) or **caldera** (Lat. *caldaria* = boiling pot). Whether you prefer the Greek derivation or the Latin, its resmblance to a kitchen vessel is unmistakable.

Volcanoes are said to be **active** (Lat. *activus* = tending to do things), **dormant** (Lat. *dormante* = asleep) or **extinct** (Lat. *extinctus* = quenched).

Activity leading to an eruption is recorded on a **seismograph** (Gk. *seismos + grapho* = earthquake writing), as are earthquakes.

A 'get me out of here' moment...

What is the difference between?

Memento (Lat. = remember) and **momentum** (Lat. *movimentum* = a large movement)?

It would have been a breeze as a tourist in Pompeii on August 23rd AD79 buying a **memento** of the volcano Vesuvius. But given that the fateful eruption happened the next day, you would have been well advised to put your memento into your pocket and to get the hell out of there before the explosion hit you with the **momentum** of several atomic bombs.

Warfare

Going to war is a dirty business, but we seem to thrive on it. Just look at the significant dates in our history from 1066 to the present. Most of them refer to battles. We seem to be a nation almost perpetually at war. I blame it on the Romans. Caesar had a pop at us in 54BC but we managed to send him and his troops packing for the next hundred years or so. Unfortunately we let our guard down and in AD43 the Emperor Claudius rolled us over big time. The Romans came and stayed for nearly four centuries. During that time they clearly taught us a lot, including plenty of stuff they had learnt from their earlier spats with the Greeks. It comes around and it goes around.

Aegis (Gk. *aigis* = the shield of the god Zeus). The word itself means a protection and we usually use it in the phrase 'under the aegis of' someone or something which is providing us with protection.

Ballistics (Gk. *ballein* = throw). The science of projectiles started with stone-throwing ancient Greeks who gradually developed large weapons to do the job for them. One of these, the ballista, a kind of crossbow, was very successfully used by Alexander the Great and then improved by the Romans to fire metal bolts or stones with great accuracy.

Belligerent (Lat. *bellum* = war + *gerere* = conduct). Pugnacious. Anybody who consistently likes a fight. So the Romans, then.

Bomb (Gk. *bombos* = hum). The Greek word describes a deep humming or buzzing noise. This makes it an **onomatopoeic** word – one that sounds like the thing it describes (Gk. *onoma* = name + *poiéo* = make).

Catapult (Gk. *kata* = against + *pallo* = throw). The Greeks used a variety of military siege engines, which were then in turn developed by the Romans into awesome machines. We tend to think of a catapult as a small hand-held implement that chucks a small weight a small distance. A Roman catapult was a sodding great wooden structure designed to throw huge rocks at anything that got in their way.

Castle (Lat. *castellum* = diminutive of *castrum*, meaning fort). The Roman *castrum* was an army camp located in a position that was designed to be pretty permanent and well defended. It worked as a large community with the army being serviced by local suppliers (including camp followers, of course) in much the same way as the medieval castle some thousand years later.

Cohort (Lat. *cohors* = company). This has become a fashionable word, particularly in education, for a like-minded group of people. The word originally defined a tenth part of a legion (the main division of the Roman army) and would typically number around 400 men. *Cohors* is also the root for the word **court** – as in courtyard – through association with the place where a cohort was billeted and trained.

Colony (Lat. *colonus* = farmer). The Roman empire was initially created as Rome conquered the peoples of the Italian peninsula. As Rome's ambitions grew to conquering other lands in Europe and North Africa, they became more astute, realising that they would not be able to police a huge empire without local support. So as the Romans conquered territory the army squaddies due for discharge would be given, as their pension from the army, a plot of land to farm. (The modern Italian for a farmer is *colona*.) Having old soldiers around meant an emergency police force was on hand but more importantly the men could bring Roman sophistication to the natives.

Contingent (Lat. *con* = with + *tangere* = touch). A separate group of the army working in reconnaisance or skirmish assaults on the enemy but keeping in touch with the main troops.

Corps (Lat. *corpus* = body). This word generally describes a body of troops selected for a particular job such as intelligence, a field hospital or air patrols. The Latin word also gives us corpse, which is what a member of a corps hopes they won't become. It also gives us **corporation** and **corporal**.

Chariot (Lat. *carrus* = a chariot). The chariot was a vehicle of warfare across the ancient world but was not so popular with the Greeks and Romans, who preferred light cavalry and heavily armed infantry. The famous statue of Boudicca or Boadicea on the Embankment by the Victorian sculptor Thomas Thornycroft demonstrates a classic piece of artistic fiction with its knife blades on the wheel hubs. These are a pure invention – imagine charging into battle like that. The only horses you are likely to harm are your own. The Latin word *carrus* is the derivation of our word **car** and the word 'chariot' is used by the French for a supermarket trolley.

Casus belli (Lat. = the reason for war). An act or situation which justifies the declaration of war. We have now lived through times when this has been a serious issue, notably the spurious claim that weapons of mass destruction existed in Iraq prior to its invasion by US-led forces.

Fort/fortress (Lat. *fortis* = strong). A fort is a strong position which is well guarded and to all intents and purposes not disimilar to a *castrum*. Certainly a place that makes the occupants feel secure. The Fort St George, a pub on Midsummer Common in Cambridge, is on indefensible, level ground and has no guards at all, making it the exception that probes the rule.

Legion (Lat. *legio* = large army unit). The legion was the principal unit of the Roman army, which in theory was made up of 6,000 men but in practice was usually around 4,000 strong. During the conquest of Britain four legions were used, the 2nd, the 9th, the 14th and the 20th.

Pax (Lat. = peace). Peace to the Romans meant that the natives were no longer revolting. As part of the Roman technique of coercion, they would do deals with the local chieftains on the basis that you can retain your local status provided you keep your tribe from attacking us... oh, and of course, you will now have the privilege of paying taxes.

PLUTO (Lat. = god of the underworld). Pluto appears elsewhere in this book under Solar System, but the word deserves a further inclusion here with reference to the second world war. As part of the preparations for the D-Day landings a series of pipelines was laid across the channel from Sandown and Dungeness to Cherbourg and Boulogne to carry petrol. It was an acronym for Pipe Line Under The Ocean.

Warfare

Province (Lat. *provincia* = sphere of duty). As the Romans conquered large areas such as southern France or Egypt, they created separate territories which were given over to be governed by Proconsuls (statesmen who had previously held the office of consul). The derivation of the word comes from the Latin *vinculum*, a chain, with the notion that the territory had to be 'put in chains' before it could be called a province. Conquered chieftains who refused to play ball were sometimes paraded in chains during triumphal processions in Rome.

Phalanx (Gk. *phalagx* = line of battle). After all this talk about the Romans at last the Greeks turn up, or, more specifically, the Macedonians, that part of Greece which gave birth to Philip and his son Alexander the Great. The phalanx was a broad line of infantry whose aim was to be so wide that its flanks could not be breached.

Rampart (Lat. *ante* = before + *parare* = prepare). This is one of those words with a modern spelling which makes it almost unrecognisable from its root words. It literally means a structure that has been well prepared as a defence against invaders.

Tactic (Gk. *taktos* = ordered). The art of laying out your forces in their best possible array. Many of the ancient commanders favoured a simple 4-4-2 system with a phalanx made up of a flat back four and four in midfield with two cavalry divisions raiding up the wings.

Veteran (Lat. *veteris* = old). When you signed up with the Roman army you were with them for life (or, of course, in many cases death). If you managed to get through unscathed there was a decent return when you reached the end of your service, which was generally after twenty-five years. The army pension was a plot of land, usually in the province where you had last served, which you could then farm as a colonist (see above) at the same time helping to spread the Latin culture to all corners of the Empire.

What is the connection between?

Sever and **severe**?
The origins of the two words are fairly different but there is a story from early British history that can provide a link. The Roman Emperor Septimius Severus, who ruled from 193 to 211, spent his last three years in Britain, at York. Some years ago archaeologists discovered around thirty bodies of Romans which had all been decapitated and buried with their heads placed between their legs in a dishonourable burial. Their heads had been **severed** (Lat. *separare* = detach) and it has been suggested that this

related to a power struggle over the succession between Severus' two warring sons, Caracalla and Geta. It would be Caracalla who prevailed but to do so he murdered the entourage of his brother in this very **severe** way (Lat. *severus* = harsh). The Emperor's name Severus was a family name probably gained by one of his ancestors renowned for his cruelty.

A bolt out of the blue

Quarrel (Lat. *querella* = complaint)

In ascending order you have complaint, spat, handbags, quarrel, battle, all-out war. In the medieval period the word quarrel was used to refer to the bolt of a crossbow. I have seen a modern crossbow tournament in a piazza in the Umbrian town of Gubbio. These crossbows are major artillery machines that propel the bolt so fast towards the target that you can barely follow its flight as it shoots across the piazza. Seriously tougher than handbags. As a medieval knight in shining armour, you wouldn't even see it coming.

The weather is one of the commonest of all topics in our general day to day conversation. So it is not surprising that our basic weather words like rain, snow, flood and wind are native words. It is when we look at the weather from a more scientific perspective that Greek and Latin come into their own.

Aurora (Lat. = the goddess of dawn). The aurora is a phenomenon that is caused by magnetic interactions in the polar atmosphere. It can be very bright, giving the impression that it is dawning. The Northern Lights or **aurora borealis** are named after *Boreas* the Greek personification of the North wind and hence anything northern.

Anticyclone (Gk. *anti* = against + *kuklos* = circle). A system of winds that rotates outwards from an area of high atmospheric pressure. A cyclone is a system of winds that rotate inwards towards an area of low atmospheric pressure. Whichever way you look at it, your fence is going to get blown over.

Atmosphere (Gk. *atmos* = vapour + *sphaira* = ball). An atmosphere is literally the gaseous envelope that surrounds a heavenly body. Our own is mostly nitrogen and oxygen. By association the word comes to be used for the environment in which we live or any pervading mood.

Weather

Climate (Gk. *klimatos* = sloped). In a world of climate change it's not a bad idea to get a handle on what climate is before it changes completely. The derivation makes sense if you think of the prevailing state of things. The way things are moving depends on the slope they are on. We are on a pretty slippery one.

Evaporation (Lat. *e* = from + *vapor* = steam). Evaporation happens when heat causes water to be released. In a weather cycle this involves ocean water evaporating to form clouds which release their water later as rain.

Isobar (Gk. *isos* = equal + *baros* = weight). An isobar is a line on a map that connects places that have the same atmospheric pressure.

Occluded front (Lat. *occludere* = shut). An occluded front is where an area of warm air meets an area of cold air in such a way that there is an upward displacement of warm air between them, which will eventually lead to a period of rain. The cold air 'shuts' out the warm air.

There are plenty of names from the classical past that still strike a chord: Alexander the Great, a diminutive man of poor health who got to be ruler of the entire known world at the age of 33. Archimedes, who we can all thank for our Eureka moment, and Nero the man who put the fiddle onto the big stage. Behind these larger than life characters are others, less well known in themselves perhaps, but whose names have given rise to phrases which hold a currency in our language that define some interesting character **archetypes**. (Archetype derives from a Greek word for a pattern or a model.)

A **Pyrrhic victory** is a term used to describe a battle which is famously won in a war that is all but lost. It's a bit like beating Man United at Old Trafford on the last day of the season, but still being relegated. Pyrrhus was a Greek king who waged several wars against the rising power of Rome and won a spectacular victory in 279 BC at Ausculum. Unfortunately, in doing so he lost the flower of his army and eventually went back home with his tail between his legs. (He didn't get promoted again the next season.)

As **Rich as Croesus** is a phrase which in all likelihood is soon to be replaced by as Rich as Bill Gates. But here we're talking BC (Before Computers). Croesus ruled a middle eastern kingdom between Greece and Persia (modern-day Iran). He spent a lot of time lavishing his wealth on the Greeks, hoping that they would help him in his fight against the Persians. They let him build temples for them of great extravagance until he asked them to send him an army, at which point they told him, very politely, to get lost.

He obviously didn't have the **Midas touch**. But would he have wanted it? Pyrrhus and Croesus were real people, Midas however is a mythical character. He saved a friend of the god Dionysus who in return granted him any wish he wanted. This is straight out of Aladdin and like any good pantomime the point of the story is that you should never take things at face value. Midas asks that everything he touches turns to gold. He soon regrets his decision as he discovers that everything he eats and drinks turns to gold as well, so he begins to starve. The story goes that the unwanted gift was washed off him into a river which, from that day, carries gold dust in its stream. There is such a river in the Middle East, which is how the story probably originated.

Dipping, not into the river, but into the legend of the Trojan War, as we must do from time to time, brings to light **Cassandra**, a name associated with being a bringer of constant bad news. Cassie, the daughter of Priam the king of Troy, was given the power of prophecy by the god Apollo in return for the promise of sexual favours. To her credit she reneged on the deal; to her misfortune, Apollo's riposte was to ensure that she would keep the power of prophecy but would always be disbelieved. She spent most of the Trojan War prophesying doom and gloom until everyone was sick of the sight of her. When, at the end of the war, she told the Trojans that it would be a disaster to bring the Wooden Horse inside the city gates, they all shouted 'Give it a rest Cassandra', and were promptly slaughtered by the Greek soldiers hiding inside it.

We often find that we are walking a fine line between success and failure. When the chips are down you really don't want a sword poised above your head held up by a single, very fine thread. **Damocles** probably found it a bit unappetising himself. A real individual, living around 400BC, he was a courtier of King Dionysius of Syracuse in Sicily. Damocles had criticised the king's good fortune at having such an easy life, so Dionysius invited him to a great banquet. As Damocles took his place at table he realised that there was a sword above his head held up by nothing more than a single horse hair put there by his host to demonstrate the precariousness of the King's position. So don't start criticising people unless you are very sure of your ground, otherwise you certainly won't enjoy dining out on the story.

Damocles found himself in a tantalising situation, but at least he had a chance to eat. Poor old **Tantalus** himself is stricken by eternal famine. One of the first mortals to dine with the immortal gods, he stupidly tried to test them by serving up his own son in a stew to see if they could recognise the flavour. His eternal punishment is to be tortured by standing in a lake that drains away whenever he tries to drink from it, and with fruit dangling above his head which is whisked out of reach whenever he stretches to grab it. Tantalus has also given his name to a secure stand for decanters with a lockable top. It is so called because the drinks are tantalisingly on show but without the key they are totally out of reach.

Tantalus' torment is to find himself with an impossible task. One level down from an impossible task is a **Herculean** one. Bring on the twelve labours of Hercules (or Herakles to give him his Greek name). Sent mad by the goddess Hera, who is out to make trouble for him, Hercules mistakenly kills his own wife and children. (In the world of myths and legends this is an easy mistake to make!) He consults the god Apollo who tells him that the only way he can expiate his guilt is to do time in the service of King Eurystheus, a well-known local hardman. As part of his sentence Hercules will have to perform twelve feats so difficult they are virtually impossible. Of the twelve labours three are quite well known. One: capturing Cerberus, the three-headed dog that guards the entrance to the underworld; Two: killing the Nemean lion (a fierce beast in the wilds of beyond); and Three: cleaning the Augean stables. The first two required almost superhuman strength but the Augean stables were another matter entirely. It would have been the RSPCA's worst nightmare – a huge stableyard that hadn't been mucked out for years. Yuk! Hercules obviously thought better of doing the job by hand and had the bright idea of diverting a couple of local rivers into the stables to do the job for him. Result! So the next time you are presented with a Herculean task it's worth remembering that it's one thing to put in all the effort, but a little bit of savvy doesn't go amiss.

Achilles Heel

Achilles was one of the great Greek heroes in the Trojan War. He performed some heroic feats in the fighting on account of the fact that he was not a normal human. His mother, the sea nymph Thetis, was a goddess, but his father, Peleus, was mortal, which meant that Achilles himself was also mortal. Yet Thetis wanted her son to be immortal, like herself, and to this end took her new baby down to the underworld of Hades to dip him in the River Styx. She believed that this would protect him against death in the real world of humans. But in doing so she made one big mistake. It was the way that she dipped him in the water that was the problem. She held him by the back of his foot so that a small part of his heel never came in contact with the water. It was the only weak part about him but it would prove costly. Towards the end of the war the Trojan hero, Paris, fired a poisoned arrow from the walls of Troy that hit Achilles in the only part of his body that was vulnerable: the heel that his mother had held when she dipped him in the River Styx. There was no saving him and he died of the wound.

So powerful has the idea behind the story always been that we still call the tendon at the back of our ankle the Achilles, and refer to any slight weakness in an otherwise strong system as its Achilles Heel.

Whose word is it anyway?

Throughout this book there are examples of Greek and Latin words that we use in our everyday language. This page contains a collection of some more Greek and Latin words that survive in their pure form today. Some have changed their meaning over the centuries while others remain exactly the same.

Acme Gk. summit

Album Lat. a white thing (very appropriate for the Beatles double white one)

Alias Lat. otherwise

Antenna Lat. yard-arm of a mast

Area Lat. level, open space

Aroma Gk. spice

Auditorium Lat. lecture room

Census Lat. census

Crux Lat. cross

Cursor Lat. runner

Exit Lat. he goes out

Habitat Lat. it inhabits

Hubris Gk. insolent pride

Ignoramus Lat. we ignore you

Index Lat. an informer

Kudos Gk. Glory

Limbo Lat. on the border

Matrix Lat. womb

Memorabilia Lat. memorable things

Moratorium Lat. delaying

Nemesis Gk. retribution

Nous Gk. mind

Onus Lat. burden

Par Lat. Equal

Plethora Gk. fullness

Pupa Lat. doll

Re: Lat. as to the thing

Whose word is it anyway?

Spectator Lat. onlooker

Spectrum Lat. an appearance

Stasis Gk. being stationary

Status Lat. standing

Super Lat. above

Terminus Lat. limit or boundary

Thesis Gk. a setting down

Trivia Lat. places where three roads meet (Education q.v.)

Verbatim Lat. word by word

Versus Lat. towards, against

Veto Lat. I forbid

Via Lat. by way of

Rostrum (Lat. = bird's beak.)

In 338BC some ships were captured by the Romans at Antium. Their prows were decorated with great bronze beaks that were used as battering rams in sea battles. When they were later decommissioned the beaks were saved and used to adorn the speaker's platform in the Forum, which was called the Rostra after them. The word rostrum, which we prefer to use today, is simply the singular form.

The majority of us work for our living in one way or another. But the different ways are pretty varied. If by working for a living we mean doing things for payment, then in my life I have worked as a choirboy, a warehouseman, a barman, an English teacher, a travel courier, a writer, a publicist...

The world of work forms the biggest backdrop for most people's lives and some of the associated words and ideas have changed very little over hundreds of years.

The word closest to the heart of every worker since time immemorial is their **salary** (Lat. *salarium* = salt ration). The salt ration was something doled out to all the people who worked for the Roman state machine... soldiers, civil servants, town criers. Of course, it was not just salt that was doled out. In the early days of the Roman Republic it was salt plus all the other necessities of life. Salt came at the top of the list because it is an important part of our diet and is a principal cooking ingredient. As the state machine developed and money came to be used as a means of payment instead of goods the word salary was superseded by the word **stipend** (Lat. *stipendium* = the pay of a soldier). The word stipend is still used, particularly with regard to public office and the clergy; we still refer to a stipendiary magistrate as one who is paid rather than being a volunteer.

The world of work

Today our workplace tends to be dominated by the **mobile** (Lat. *mobilis* = easy to move) and the **computer** (Lat. *computare* = calculate). Our desktop is full of **icons** (Gk. *eikón* = image) and we constantly need to put our **cursor** (Lat. = runner) in the right place on our **monitor** (Lat. = an advisor). The word cursor was originally used to describe the movable upright bar used to line up the notches on a slide rule, while a monitor was someone who reminds or warns, which is probably why my monitor gives me so many error messages. Still useful is the fax machine. Fax is a shortened form of the word **facsimile** (Lat. *fac* = make + *simile* = like). The Latin word *fac* can also mean do. For many years, as a freelance writer I traded under the name of **factotum** (Lat. *fac* = do + *totum* = all) as an indication that I would do anything a client wanted (within reason!). The title factotum was used in the middle ages to describe a private secretary.

Of course, any self respecting organisation has to have a **logo** (Gk. *logos* = word) to ensure that it makes the right **impression** (Lat. *impressus* = the imprint of a seal).

Companies belong to the world of **commerce** and **industry** (Lat. *commercium* = trade and *industria* = diligence). The Romans used the word *commercium* in warfare to describe negotiations about the ransoms of prisoners. In the commercial world everything is organised on a **fiscal** basis (Lat. *fiscus* = a wallet). By the time of the Roman Empire the *fiscus* had become the name used to describe the state treasury. Successful companies make **profits** (Lat. *proficere* = gain ground) and **distribute** them (Lat. *distributus* = asigned) as **dividends** (Lat. *dividendum* = to be divided up). If we are lucky, from time to time, we may get a **bonus** (Lat. = a good thing).

As a taxi-driver, hair stylist or waiter you may get a tip or **gratuity** (Lat. *gratuitus* = not paid for, spontaneous). When we retire from work we will need a **pension** (Lat. *pensio* = a weighing out for payment).

In the workplace we may have a secretary and we will certainly have colleagues. The word **secretary** (Lat. *secretus* = set apart) was originally used to describe someone who dealt with a public official's private affairs, set apart from their public activities. And although we think of **colleagues** as being our equals they weren't originally. The Latin word *collegatus* meant to be appointed as a deputy, or made your second-in-command. Probably best not to make this too obvious to any of your colleagues.

A group of people with a common link is sometimes

referred to as a **nexus**, a Latin word which means a binding or tying together.

And as if all this work wasn't tiring enough, there's the ever-present taxman to contend with, including the dreaded officials who work for Customs and **Excise** (Lat. *excisus* = a piece cut out). Ouch!

Yellow Pages

Take a walk down any high street and you will find plenty of trades that have their origins in Greek and Latin words.

Antique dealer (Lat. *antiquus* = ancient). *Antiquus* is related to *ante*, meaning before. The Romans also used the word to describe people of previous times.

Barber (Lat. *barba* = beard). The Romans were fastidious about their appearance and spent much of their leisure time at the public baths where a barber might have a small salon for shaving gentlemen. In our modern world, as we find it easy to shave ourselves but less easy to cut our own hair, the barber is less likely to be a beard trimmer and is more often a haircutter.

Florist (Lat. *floris* = of a flower). Our love affair with flowers is as old as the hills. They've long been used as personal adornments, decorations in the home and as love tokens.

Funeral Director (Lat. *funeris* = of burial). Roman funerals were elaborate rituals like our own. Hired mourners would precede the body, laid out on a bier, to the place of cremation. A coin was placed under the tongue to pay Charon, the ferryman, to take the departed soul across the river Styx to the sanctuary of the underworld. The ashes were then put in an urn which was buried.

Mechanic (Gk. *mékhané* = inventive). The word comes from Greek, meaning any artificial device or contrivance, particularly an engine of war and thus the people who worked with it. So we should stop looking down on mechanics as grease-monkeys and give them the status they deserve. Except the ones whose bills are clearly artificial contrivances.

Pharmacy (Gk. *pharmakon* = drug). The word applies both to the preparation and the dispensing of drugs.

Photographer (Gk. *phótos* = of light + *graphó* = write). A photograph used to be the result of light creating chemical reactions on sensitive film. Today, the digital camera is no longer making a chemical reaction but performing a computerised digital operation. We all think we're great photographers but from time to time we do need to call in the professionals. You can hardly take the photographs at your own wedding, can you?

Printer (Lat. *premit* = he presses). A print is literally a mark that has been produced by pressing a template on to a base substance. In the world of modern printing, **lithography** is the word used (Gk. *lithos* = stone + *graphó* = write). The idea comes from a stone or metal surface which has been engraved so that only the raised areas accept the ink which is then pressed onto the paper or card.

The signs of the Zodiac are well known and the majority of us know our own star sign. The word is derived from the Greek *zóion* meaning animal. There seems to be an insatiable demand in our media for **horoscopes** (Gk. *hóra* = time + *skopos* = observer). The signs of the Zodiac demonstrate a pure example of how Latin is alive in our modern language since all bar two of the signs are Latin words. The two exceptions are Libra and Capricorn. Libra is the plural of the Latin word for a pound weight, used with scales, but not the scales themselves, and Capricorn is not just a goat but specifically one with horns.

Aries (Lat. = ram) March 21-April 20
Planet: Mars. Arians are go-getters with lots of energy and competitiveness. They don't suffer fools gladly and don't take criticism well. Often cheerful, they have a spontaneity which makes them fun friends.
Famous Arieans: Elton John, Emma Thompson, Emperor Caracalla.
Taurus (Lat. = bull) April 21-May 21
Planet: Venus. Taureans are practical, hard-working and love money and the comfort it can bring for them and those around them. But stubborn! They like responsibility and take a non-hostile approach, but hate cheats.

Famous Taureans: David Beckham, Shakespeare, Emperor Marcus Aurelius.

Gemini (Lat. = twins) May 22-June 21

Planet: Mercury. There are two sides to every Gemini, great fun but prone to be unreliable. Generous, impulsive and always looking for something new. Good parents, their houses are likely to be full of books, CDs and the latest technology.

Famous Geminis: Bob Dylan, Liz Hurley, JFK, Henry VIII, Germanicus (father of Emperor Caligula).

Cancer (Lat. = crab) June 22-July 23

Planet: Moon. Cancerians can be rather secretive. They love security but also seek adventure. They like the sound of their own voice and make excellent sales people. They have a feel for history and tend to have good memories.

Famous Cancerians: Tom Hanks, George Michael, Julius Caesar, Alexander the Great.

Leo (Lat. = lion) July 24-August 23

Planet: Sun. These Kings and Queens of the savannah want to be top dog or cat in whatever they do. They're very generous, extremely helpful and enjoy being with people. Proud to live in a pride you might say.

Famous Leos: Monica Lewinsky, Bill Clinton, Napoleon, Emperor Claudius.

Virgo (Lat. = virgin) August 24-September 23
Planet: Mercury. Virgos want everything to be perfect.
They're inquisitive, intelligent and make fantastic friends,
capable of sorting out other people's crises with the
minimum of fuss. Can be shy so turn to practical areas of
life like acting and sport.

*Famous Virgos: Hugh Grant, Elizabeth I, Emperor Augustus,
Emperor Caligula.*

Libra (Lat. = pounds) September 24-October 23
Planet: Venus. Affectionate, sympathetic and very interested
in people. Librans have a great desire for self-expression and
although they may be shy they have great leadership
qualities and have a keen sense of fair play.

*Famous Librans: Kate Winslett, John Lennon, Nelson,
Virgil, Pompey.*

Scorpio (Lat. = scorpion) October 24-November 22
Planet: Pluto. Scorpios are reliable, resourceful and full of
self belief. Loyal and honest, they don't like change and are
easily hurt but will never show it. They prefer to be the
power behind the throne rather than in the limelight.

*Famous Scorpios: Julia Roberts, Churchill, Emperors
Domitian and Tiberius.*

The Zodiac

Sagitarius (Lat. = archer) November 23-December 21
Planet: Jupiter. Sagitarians really love life and have very open personalities. Broad minded, the life and soul of the party they have a penchant for speaking the truth. Their values are spiritual rather than material and they don't enjoy being tied down by responsibility.
Famous Sagittarians: Billy Connolly, Jane Austen, Emperor Nero, Horace.

Capricorn (Lat. *capri* = goat + *cornu* = horn) December 22-January 20 Planet:
Saturn. Capricorns tend to retain their youthful good looks throughout life and are very down to earth. They never shun family responsibilities, are easily embarassed and don't like to annoy others. They have genuine kindness and a good sense of humour.
Famous Capricorns: Tiger Woods, David Bowie, Cicero, Mark Antony.

Aquarius (Lat. = of water) January 21-February 19
Planet: Saturn. Original, inventive and smart, Aquarians make friends easily but can be more comfortable with ideals than with day-to-day routine. Many make good teachers but can be a little eccentric as they enjoy being different.

Famous Aquarians: Paul Newman, Vanessa Redgrave, Lord Byron, Emperor Hadrian.

Pisces (Lat. = fishes) February 20-March 20

Planet: Neptune. Kind, thoughtful, clever and caring, Pisceans are capable of reaching the top but often don't. They feel insecure yet they will always make sacrifices for others. They are everyone's friend and can never say no.

Famous Pisceans: Liza Minelli, Michael Caine, Vivaldi, Ovid.

Zoo time

The zoo is a Victorian invention, originally called a **zoological** garden. (Gk. *zóion* = living thing + *logos* = knowledge). The first zoos were a mixture of **flora** (Lat. = goddess of flowers) and **fauna** (Lat. = goddess of woodland animals). Eventually the fauna won out and the flora moved to **botanical** gardens (Gk. *botanikos* = of plants) and **arboretums** (Lat. *arbor* = tree).

These days, zoos encompass most living animals, even spiders and scorpions, which go by the name of **arachnids** (Gk. *arakhné* = spider). If we do have a bit of a phobia we can quickly move on to the birdhouse or **aviary** (Lat. *avis* = bird). One of the most colourful is the kingfisher, called by the Greeks *alkuón*, from which we get the term **Halcyon** days, meaning a period of prosperity. This was originally fourteen days around the middle of winter when the bird was thought to breed. On the other side of the coin are the **raptors** (Lat. *raptor* = plunderer), including all the **falcons** (Lat. *falconis* = scythelike), named after the shape of their beak.

In the snake house are the boas and pythons. The **boa** takes its name from the Greek for a cow, *bous*. According to Pliny, a Roman who wrote works on natural history, it was believed that the snake sucked the milk of cows. Any self-respecting cow would do well to ignore Pliny since if the boa was a **constrictor** (Lat. *constrictum* = bound fast) the cow was in a decidedly dodgy position. The **python** takes its name from Greek mythology, the *Puthon* being a huge serpent slain by Apollo near Delphi. Also from Greek myth comes the word **dragon** (Gk. *drakón* = one who watches), referring to the monster that guarded the golden apples in the garden of the Hesperides, a beautiful mythical place believed to be situated in the Atlas mountains.

If we move to the African enclosure we'll find the **elephants** (Gk. *elephantos*), **camels** (Gk. *kamélos*) and the **rhinoceros** (Gk. *rhinos* = nose + *kerós* = horn). The Greek *rhino-* stem gives us words in medicine that refer to the nose, such as **rhinoplasty** (or nosejob). This is also where you'll find the **hippopotamus**, made up of the two Greek words for horse and river. The hippos, rhinos and elephants are all **pachyderms**, again from two Greek words for thick and skin. So the next time you want to refer to someone as being thick-skinned just call them a pachyderm.

The African plains are home to the big cats, and as the Greeks didn't travel much into Africa their understanding wasn't all it might have been. The Greek word *león* was clearly a **lion** but after that they begin to go off the rails. The **panther** (Gk. *pan* = all + *théra* = beasts) was so called because it was thought that the animal was friendly with all creatures (great and small) except the dragon. It was also called a *pardos* and the **leopard** was thought to be a cross between the pard and the lion. Another african animal they made a bit of a horlicks of naming was the **crocodile**. The Greeks encountered these creatures in the Nile and called them *krokodeilos*, made up of two words meaning the purple crocus and coward. The last thing you want to call a crocodile is a coward that looks like a purple crocus – it'll eat you alive!

The reptile house is home to the **lizards** (Lat. *lacerta* = a tearing to pieces, a word which also gives us **lacerate**). One of the lizards is the salamander. The Greek salamander was a mythical lizard that could live in fire which it quenched by the chill of its body, all **reptiles** being cold-blooded (Lat. *reptilis* = crawling).

Finally we reach the **marsupials** (Lat. *marsuppium* = a purse). This is just the sort of way you can imagine Kanga explaining things to Roo, 'Now come on, hop back into my purse and we can go and find tigger'. I nearly forgot **tigger** (Gk. *tigris*), where the Greeks were quite sure of their facts, probably through contact with Asia rather than Africa. Like many of the other animals the tiger is a **quadruped** (Lat. *quadrupedis* = with four feet).

Zoo time

Depending on the time of year you visit, some of the animals might have gone into **hibernation,** from the Latin *hibernare*, a word relating to the army practice of going into winter quarters after the campaining season was over. Some animals go to sleep for the whole of the summer. They are said to **aestivate** (Lat. *aestivare* = pass the summer). Examples are some crocodile and frog species. You'll rarely see some animals, the **nocturnal** ones, that only come out at night (Lat. *nocturnus* = by night).

Step into the aquarium and you'll find an array of nice things to eat. First on the menu are the **molluscs** (Lat. *mollis* = soft) and the **crustaceans** (Lat. *crustaceus* = covered with a shell). The molluscs include mussels, cockles, whelks, etc. The crustaceans are the crabs, lobsters, shrimps and the like. Given that they all have soft edible flesh and live in shells, you could be forgiven for wondering what the difference is. The ability to move, I think. The molluscs don't, the crustaceans do. And moving on we find the **cephalopods** (Gk. *kephalé* + *podos* = head with feet), which are a strange looking bunch with big heads and straggly appendages, like the cuttlefish and the **octopus** (Gk. *októ* + *pous* = eight foot). Then there are the **gastropods** (Gk. *gastero* + *podos* = stomach foot), the family of snails and their cousins. They get their name from their way of walking since the locomotive organ is joined to their stomachs.

Before we leave let's give an apology to the **porpoise**, which very unfairly is named from two Latin words, *porcus* and *piscis*, meaning pig fish.

Sorry about that, porpoise.

INDEX
Index

Index

Index

Nigel P. Brown   339

Index

Index

Index

Index

Index

Index

Index

Index

Index